A Clan Mother's Call

SUNY series in Critical Haudenosaunee Studies

Kevin J. White, editor

Ionkwathroriiannions Ionkwakara'shon:'a

We are telling our own stories

~

A Clan Mother's Call

Reconstructing Haudenosaunee Cultural Memory

Jeanette Rodriguez

with Iakoiane Wakerahkats:teh,
Condoled Bear Clan Mother of the Kanien'kehá:ka Nation

Cover image: *Woman's Nomination*, by Brandon Lazore, courtesy of the artist

Published by State University of New York Press, Albany

For information, contact State University of New York Press, Albany, NY
www.sunypress.edu

Production, Eileen Nizer
Marketing, Michael Campochiaro

Library of Congress Cataloging-in-Publication Data

Names: Rodriguez, Jeanette, 1954– | Wakerahkats:teh, Iakoiane.
Title: A clan mother's call : reconstructing Haudenosaunee cultural memory / Jeanette Rodriguez, Ph.D. ; with Iakoiane Wakerahkats:teh, Condoled Bear Clan Mother of the Kanien'kehá:ka Nation.
Description: Albany : State University of New York Press, 2017. | Series: SUNY series in critical Haudenosaunee studies | Includes bibliographical references and index.
Identifiers: LCCN 2016041496 (print) | LCCN 2017017894 (ebook) | ISBN 9781438466255 (ebook) | ISBN 9781438466231 (hardcover : alk. paper) | ISBN 9781438466248 (pbk. : alk. paper)
Subjects: LCSH: Iroquois Indians. | Wakerakatste, Iakoiane. | Iroquois women—Biography. | Iroquois Indians—Social life and customs. | Mohawk women—Biography. | Mohawk Indians—Social life and customs. | Indian women—North America—History. | Sex role—North America. | Indians of North America—Rites and ceremonies.
Classification: LCC E99.I7 (ebook) | LCC E99.I7 R584 2017 (print) | DDC 974.7004/9755—dc23
LC record available at https://lccn.loc.gov/2016041496

10 9 8 7 6 5 4 3 2 1

We dedicate this book to all indigenous daughters of the earth so that they can inherit our world without persecution, and that their creator-given gift to bring forth life is returned to a place of high honor. And to our sons, we return you to your primal role of protector so that you may stand in balance during this time of great renewal.

A nation is not conquered until the hearts of its women are on the ground. Then it is done, no matter how brave its warriors nor how strong their weapons.

—Cheyenne proverb

The phenomenon of the Indian heart is unyielding in its ability to survive and to endlessly hold a love for the land we regard as our mother and we as her children.

—Iakoiane Wakerahkats:teh, Condoled Bear Clan Mother of the Kanien'kehá:ka Nation

This is to be strong of mind, O chiefs: Carry no anger and hold no grudges. Think not forever of yourselves, O chiefs, nor of your own generations. Think of the continuing generations of our families, think of our grandchildren and of those yet unborn, whose faces are coming from beneath the ground.

—The Peacemaker

Contents

Acknowledgments

A book that enters the heart of a People could not be written without the generosity of the People themselves sharing who they are, their hopes, and aspirations.

I begin these acknowledgments by first giving thanks to Iakoiane Wakerahkats:teh, Bear Clan Matron of the Kanien'kehá:ka (Mohawk) Nation at Akwesasne, for opening her heart and community to me. I thank all the Kanien'kehá:ka women and men who took the time to share their stories and vision; these tales were always heart-filled, inspiring, and were at times also difficult to share. It is this willingness to share from a deep, heartfelt place that provides the bridge for various communities to engage one another. Trust is a fragile entity that takes a long time to build.

The material in this book adds another voice to the literature and scholarship about the Haudenosaunee—but from a distinctive Haudenosaunee source. As such, I am grateful for the risk that Iakoiane Wakerahkats:teh took in allowing me to come into her community's land and transcribe her thoughts. Indigenous peoples are distrustful of "others" for two reasons: first, outsiders have historically entered their communities and taken without giving back; second, indigenous communities have largely been misrepresented, especially when it comes to women's roles within the nation. For these reasons and more, I am incredibly grateful for the trust extended to me, especially given the resistance that both Iakoiane Wakerahkats:teh and I encountered during the creation of the book. I come upon the Haudenosaunee land in a spirit of humility, knowing that I am neither of the Kanien'kehá:ka Nation nor their traditions. I come as a scholar of religion and culture, desiring to gain both an intellectual and experiential understanding of the Kanien'kehá:ka.

I am appreciative of Dean Powers of Seattle University for granting me the Dean's Faculty Fellowship Grant and Dr. Ted Fortier, director of Canadian Studies at Seattle University, both of whom provided the financial support that made my fieldwork possible. I also wish to thank my friends and colleagues, Drs. Sharon Callahan, Christi Eppler, James Hembree, Nalini Iyer, and Christina Roberts, for their insights, questions, and critiques during the writing of this book. I am grateful for the commitment of my exemplary research assistant, Lauren Woo-Ermacoff, who has dedicated over three years of her time to this project. Her keen intellect, sharp eyes, and nimble fingers transcribed tapes, analyzed documents, and edited this manuscript. I am additionally extremely thankful to Nancy Marshall and Lauren St. Pierre for their continuous efforts, as well as my wonderful student research assistants Danielle Winslow and Tori Head, who demonstrated enthusiasm, skill, and patience while reviewing documents; and Amanda Lanne-Camilli and Chelsea Miller at the State University of New York Press. What I appreciated most about those who assisted in this project was not only their skill and competency to do the research, but their enthusiasm and openness to the subject matter. They exemplify the next generation: eager to learn and seek reconciliation.

Finally, research is made easier with the help of librarians and archivists willing to assist in finding potentially lost documents. For this, I wish to thank Rose Chou, reference archivist at the National Anthropological Archives at the Smithsonian Institution, and reference librarians Karen Gilles and Mary Sepulveda from Seattle University.

Introduction

The Call of the Earth Mother

For the first time in six hundred years, humanity has arrived at a juncture where women can define their distinct perspective of her/history. Through women's writings and traditions their important and individual perspectives are brought to the surface. It is important to offer a woman-centered view of her/history and the world in which we live because the traditionally feminine values of interdependence, mutuality, and respect will help to reshape our society and response to the global environmental crisis.

This book explores issues centered on empowerment in indigenous communities through the transmission of ancestral knowledge. Ancient wisdom has been used to heal the Mohawk nation as witnessed in the Haudenosaunee[1] (Mohawk) territory of Akwesasne. It is my privilege to have encountered and grown in friendship with women from Haudenosaunee (Iroquois) territories in New York, Ontario, and Quebec. Transcribing and reflecting upon the teachings and counsel of traditional Kanien'kehá:ka Clan Mother Iakoiane Wakerahkats:teh, this book explores her leadership roles and responsibilities as Bear Clan Mother, which include the transformation of ancient traditions into contemporary practices.

Iakoiane[2] Wakerahkats:teh is a Condoled[3] Bear Clan Mother[4] and sits on the Mohawk Nation Council of Chiefs and Clan Mothers in Akwesasne, a vast territory comprised of twelve thousand Mohawks living along the St. Lawrence River in northern New York.[5] As Clan Mother, Iakoiane Wakerahkats:teh plays a pivotal role in selecting and raising her nation's leaders and facilitates Crossover Ceremonies for the young, which are rituals of transitions through the life stages. While her main responsibility is for the welfare of the clan, Iakoiane Wakerahkats:teh also bestows ancestral names to the people under her lineage. Her role in the installation and removal of male chiefs is confirmed in the constitution Kianenrehsehrah:kowa (the Great Law of Peace).[6] Through her guidance and with the support of the "aunties" and "uncles" of her community, the traditional Crossover Ceremonies have been pulled from the Earth to be practiced again in Akwesasne. The Clan Mother contends that key to this process is passing on the knowledge that allows indigenous youths to be in balance with themselves, their community, and their environment.

I have previously explored and researched the roles, development, and transformation of women within the complex issues of identity, culture, and the transmission of collective/cultural memory. In this case, I am focusing on cultural memory that sustains resilience. Many indigenous communities globally evidence the important role of women as the source and transmitters of cultural wisdom and knowledge. This role makes women vital to the survival of their community.[7] My personal interest in the Bear Clan (Mohawk) Mother is best understood through my identity as a mestiza.[8] Due to my mixed-race heritage, I have had a longstanding commitment to understanding the navigation and articulation of issues of identity for those of us who find ourselves positioned in two or more worlds at the same time.

I met Clan Mother Iakoiane Wakerahkats:teh (whose Okwehon:we name means "resilient snowflake") in 2009, through the American Indian Institute (AII) located in Bozeman, Montana. The AII is a modern Indian Circle that provides administration, funding, development, and program support to advance the work and vision of the Traditional Circle. This Traditional Circle brings together elders and non-Indians who are dedicated to the survival of indigenous heritages by supporting indigenous peoples and the issues that they find most important. Indigenous women are particularly active within the Traditional Circle:

> No matter where indigenous women gather or for what purpose, they almost always talk about family and community and express concern about traditional values, culture, and lifeways slipping away. It is the women who are responsible for bringing along the next generation to carry the culture forward.[9]

When speaking of indigenous efforts to preserve their culture, it is imperative to keep in mind that until 1978 many Native Americans were forbidden from teaching their culture and languages in schools or even from practicing their ceremonies. In fact, many indigenous individuals were persecuted for continuing to practice their ceremonies.

Approximately fifty elders and non-Indian people nationwide gather annually with the purpose of sharing indigenous traditions and identifying common concerns. The indigenous perspective is defined by its holistic view of the environment and social structure; it is a spiritual voice that integrates the emotional, mental, physical, and spiritual world vision of Native Americans. There is no dichotomy between reality and spirituality, as what is commonly perceived in the Western world as spirituality defines the indigenous way of life. Thus, much of what the Clan Mother shares in the following pages is founded in a "radically different paradigm from that which many readers, including myself, bring to this book."[10] This foundation is differentiated by its "continual openness to learning something new and unknown," as opposed to pursuing the certainty of having a correct and quantifiable answer.[11] There is an increasing sense of urgency and importance in having these gatherings. Thus far, the forums have been hosted by different indigenous communities: the Anishinaabe in Bemidji (2006), the Haida Gwaii in British Columbia (2007), the Salish/Kootenai/Pend D'Oreille at the Flathead Indian Reservation in Montana (2008), the Navajo near Canyon de Chelly (2009), the Haudenosaunee at the Kanatsiohareke Kanien'kehá:ka Community (2011), and the Pueblo at Ghost Ranch, Santa Fe (2013). Over the years, participants have had the opportunity to meet with elders and discuss issues as far ranging as sustainability, women's ways of knowing, youth, and laws and treaties.

In August 2010, I was invited to attend a powerful gathering of Haudenosaunee (Iroquois) Mohawk Nation Territory at Akwesasne. This gathering, entitled Life Blood of Our Nations, was an awe-inspiring congregation of Haudenosaunee women across the confederacy who journeyed together, sharing revealing stories about their current conditions and lives. It also marked a rare occasion when the Haudenosaunee women allowed individuals outside the clan to enter the heart of their Nation. The gathering consisted of over one hundred native women, and its purpose was to direct, organize, and implement the articulation and dissemination of indigenous women's authoritative message of cultural transmission. Their goal was to create a global message and to join with other indigenous communities around the world to address the various injustices perpetrated against their peoples. In order to actualize their goal, together they retrieved and recalled their role within their history.

> Embracing the role of keepers of culture, contemporary Native American women are taking responsibility for maintaining the heart of their traditional cultures against the TV age. Many are attempting to maintain circles of their Native communities in the midst of urban sprawl, provide their children with tribal identity to help them resist assimilating pressures of public school, and even bridge the chasm for Natives who had no

> Native upbringing. The tasks may have changed, but the work of being a Native American woman is as challenging as ever. Native American women will persevere, as they have for thousands of years, in an imperfect world, shaping life out of what is there.[12]

At the top of the women's agenda was an appeal for consideration of the earth. The following is one among the many indigenous voices emerging globally in defense of Mother Earth:

> As indigenous people, our lives are intertwined with the natural world . . . we are all co-equal beings sharing the gifts of our sacred Mother Earth. We are dependent upon her for our sustenance, interdependent upon one another for the fulfillment of our lives and interconnected with one another spiritually and ethically.[13]

While there are many differences among the varying indigenous groups within the United States, there is, "among traditional people[,] a fundamental understanding that everything is related and that all living things play an important role in keeping the Earth in balance."[14] In addition,

> Over 95 percent of the world's high-biodiversity areas overlap with lands claimed by indigenous peoples, partly because biodiversity is central to indigenous sustenance and ecological management strategies, and partly because indigenous lands have not been subject to the intensive development and industrialization that has destroyed biodiversity elsewhere. As a result, today indigenous peoples are traditional stewards of 90 percent of the Earth's remaining biodiversity, even as they make up 90 percent of its cultural diversity.[15]

As a result of these gatherings and my growing relationship with the Clan Mother, I became sensitized to Iakoiane Wakerahkats:teh's need to have her teachings put in an accessible format that would allow the emerging generations of young Haudenosaunee to follow their ancestors' wisdom. The Clan Mother had begun to question how rooted Haudenosaunee young were in their cultural memory. In more academic terms, the Clan Mother was posing the question: "How does the ancient knowledge and tradition of indigenous peoples offer practical insights into where we are, and how to proceed forward?"

Iakoiane Wakerahkats:teh invited me to convey her vision as a written record that would animate her nation's continued commitment to reclaim their voice, authority, land, and hope (see appendix 1). Like Paige Rabmon before me, I too believe that "when Indigenous individuals seek input from collaborators in order to share their knowledge and histories in written forms . . . it is both intellectually justified and ethically imperative to employ scholarly platforms to amplify their voices."[16] For my part, this was an opportunity to engage in a meaningful conversation and to explore the indigenous way of life and spirituality as a genuine and distinctive truth. Working alongside the Clan Mother allowed me to explore how these indigenous ways of being might be related to my own tradition and subsequently find a point of interconnection.

Iakoiane Wakerahkats:teh was aware of my work with indigenous communities in the global south (*Cultural Memory: Resistance, Faith and Identity* [2007]) with my coauthor, Dr. Ted Fortier. I also had the opportunity to share with her my own background as a mestiza, the daughter of a Spanish-Ecuadorian father and an Indian (Quechua)-Ecuadorian mother. Although my mother died when I was young and I did not have the opportunity to learn about the formidable and ancient people of the Andes, I have always felt a recognition, a comradery, and a desire to learn more of Indian ways, for we as indigenous people do share in some core values, such as respect, balance, coexistence, and gratitude to a Creator.

One strength of indigenous cultures comes from the understanding not only of the conscious nature of the earth, her elements, and the directions but also the unity and interrelationship between all creation. I remember hearing about the prophecy of the eagle and the condor as a little girl. The prophecy spoke of the time when there would be peace, and this new age would begin when the eagle and the condor jointly took to the skies in flight. The encounter of the condor and the eagle was addressed during the First Encounter of Okwehon:we (Indigenous) Peoples in Quito, Ecuador, in 1990. The significance of the union between the condor and eagle is its symbolic representation of the union of the native peoples of North and South America. Ten years later in 2000, indigenous and nonindigenous peoples gathered in the Guatemalan mountains near Tikal in fulfillment of an ancient prophecy: the long-awaited meeting of the Eagle (representing the indigenous peoples of North America) and the Condor (representing the indigenous peoples of South America).

As I reflect now, I was extraordinarily fortunate to be invited to participate in the American Indian Institute Elder gatherings. The gatherings offered me an opportunity to witness and learn from the vehicles that native peoples around the world utilize to reconnect as described in the prophecy of the condor and the eagle. The strategies include visiting other communities, sometimes across continents, participating in journey runs, planning elder-youth encounters, organizing around specific issues such as land, human rights, health, education, treaty issues, and addressing the international community through the United Nations. This book records the mediums that Iakoiane Wakerahkats:teh and the Haudenosaunee people opened to me so that others could visit, participate, and organize toward rebuilding the Haudenosaunee people.

As I proceeded deeper into more intimate conversations with Iakoiane Wakerahkats:teh, I became aware of three significant starting points. One, there has been no precedence—contemporary or historical—of a native Clan Mother articulating her teachings and experiences in the first person. My intent is both to record Iakoiane Wakerahkats:teh's teachings for the purpose of rebuilding her nation and to engage with her in a meaningful conversation. It is for this reason that this book does not attempt to address a research question but, instead, weaves a narrative around the Clan Mother's desire to impart Haudenosaunee traditions and lessons to a larger audience. When I speak of teachings, I am describing the Haudenosaunee "ways, beliefs, values, and practices" recounted by the Clan Mother and recorded by myself within this book.[17] As Paige Rabmon notes, these teachings do not belong to any individual but are rather the communal possession of the Haudenosaunee.[18]

Second, because of my work in Latin America, I am aware that many indigenous people feel they must articulate themselves as subject. Engaging Native Americans or indigenous people is not reviewing the history of a people that exist*ed* but a people who remain alive, living and transmitting their identities, values, hopes, and aspirations through culture. Reawakening the seeds of indigenous culture is an essential part of cultural healing, which is imperative for native communities that were so damaged and affected by colonization. Despite these continual assaults on their way of life, indigenous people demonstrate a resilience we are only now beginning to understand.

> The peoples that exist today are the people that were there from the beginning . . . they have been what they are today since that time, but they have carried many years, many decades, many centuries of being disposed and pushed aside . . . yet they are still alive and their life is not only simply their life, but life capable of saving the life of others . . .[19]

The preceding sentiments from "The VI Latin America Encounter of Pastoral and Solidarity Work with Indigenous Peoples" may be echoed in indigenous communities in North America as well. Stories have the potential to deliver helpful and even healing knowledge, and it is for this reason that the Clan Mother has invited me to work with her on this endeavor. Thus, the reader is encouraged to explore the Clan Mother's teachings, which "are not a set of abstract ideas but principles for living that should be practiced and passed on."[20]

Third, the fundamental ethnographic data collection techniques employed for this project were interviews, archival work, and participant observation. I am grateful to have been given permission to do the ethnographic work in Akwesasne because it granted me the ability to observe the behavior of the community within everyday situations, such as within ceremonies. According to Dr. Angrosino, professor of anthropology at the University of South Florida, "the primary ethical responsibility of any ethnographic research is to respect the dignity and the privacy of those being studied."[21] In observance of this responsibility, let me note that participant observation is not simply a matter of living close to the people one studies, nor is it just the collection of data. Rather, participant observation is "a way of thinking about the people from whom one collects those data. It is also a way in which one perceives one's own position in relation to the people and the culture one is studying."[22] Having said that, I am mindful that ethnographic writing and methods will be limited "to our poor reach of mind, to notions of our day and time, crude, partial, and confined."[23]

As I engaged with and reflected upon the Haudenosaunee people and their rituals of initiation and identity, I became mindful of three major contributions that the Haudenosaunee people have made to the inhabitants of Turtle Island (North America): first, the Haudenosaunee have sustained their cultural knowledge against great odds; second, the role of Haudenosaunee women exercising power over property and their own bodies acted as an impetus for the United States' women's rights movement; and third, the Haudenosaunee lead the environmental movement by example through their continued respect and nurturance toward Mother Earth.

We can trace the fundamental roots of our democracy to the early governance of the Haudenosaunee Confederacy: "In October 1988, the United States Congress passed concurrent resolutions acknowledging the contribution of the Iroquois Confederacy and the Great Law to the development of the confederation of the original thirteen colonies and the United States Constitution."[24] The Haudenosaunee are a centuries-old confederacy comprised of different Okwehon:we (Indigenous) nations: Kanien'kehá:ka (Possessors of the Flint), Oneniote'a:ka (People of the Standing Stone),

Ononta'keha:ka (People on Top of the Hills), Kaion'keha:ka (People of the Mucky Land), and Shotinontowane'a:ka (Keepers of the Western Door).[25] The Tehatiskaro:ros (Shirt-Wearing People) were later adopted into the confederacy, thus forming "The Six Nations."[26] As an ancient people living in the modern world, the Haudenosaunee are confronted with many complex issues, such as attempting to heal from historical and multigenerational traumas that encompass disease, loss of language and land, stereotyping, and poverty, among others. Despite these issues, and both government and religious pressure to assimilate, there continues to exist a well-guarded fountain of cultural knowledge.

The development of North American feminism emerged specifically as a result of witnessing the position, role, and influence Haudenosaunee women occupied within their Nation. In fact, the early United States women's rights movement was born in the territory of the Haudenosaunee in 1848. Feminist pioneer Dr. Sally Roesch Wagner has written about this early influence, focusing her attention on Matilda Joslyn Gage, one of the three main leaders in the movement along with Elizabeth Cady Stanton and Lucretia Mott. It was Gage who wrote extensively about the Haudenosaunee women, "Especially the position of women in what she termed their 'matriarchate' or system of 'mother-rule.'"[27] Gage evidences her case by asserting that the Haudenosaunee provided early American feminists with the model of freedom for women that at that time they themselves were not experiencing. Within the six nations in the confederacy, Haudenosaunee women were visible and wielded great political power, control of their property, custody of their children, and dominion over their bodies. Onondaga Nation Deer Clan Mother Audrey Shenandoah stated the following in 2000 at the annual Elizabeth Cady Stanton birthday tea in Seneca Falls, New York:

> Iroquois women continue to have the responsibility of nominating, counseling, and keeping in office the male chief who represents the clan in the grand council. In the six nations of the Iroquois confederacy, Haudenosaunee women have worked with the men to successfully guard their sovereign political status against persistent attempts to turn them into United States citizens. We have always had these responsibilities.[28]

Now, over 150 years later, we have another opportunity to learn from Haudenosaunee women in terms of the significance of the reclaiming and nurturing of our relationship with the earth. As Eric Noyes, executive director of the American Indian Institute, states:

> Indigenous wisdom, or original spiritual teachings, indeed can serve as vital touchstones for human behavior, ethics, and lifeways. The wisdom carried in the breast of the Indian spiritual leaders reminds us of the reality that human beings are part of an undivided wholeness with the natural world. Their worldview is the doorway back to the earth.[29]

This book will focus specifically on Iakoiane Wakerahkats:teh in her role as Clan Mother and her commitment to reinvigorate her community's ancestral wisdom through crossover rituals. Her desire is to bring young people to a place of original instruction and spiritual connection for, as she says, "Children cannot know who they want to be if they do not know where they came from."[30] Her sentiments are further echoed by Taiaiake Alfred, a Kanien'kehá:ka educator, activist, and author: "To preserve what is left of our cultures and lands is a constant fight. . . . The only way we can survive is to recover our strength, our wisdom, and our solidarity by honoring and revitalizing the core of our traditional teachings."[31]

It is my hope that the openness to this ancestral knowledge will offer all of us insights into the contemporary challenges of inclusion, democracy, and sustainability within Native American communities and our own. As this study offers a unique perspective on the role of a traditional Clan Mother from the Akwesasne Mohawk community, the introduction concludes with the Call of the Bear Clan Mother.

The first chapter provides the context from which this research was conducted. It includes a discussion of the personal invitation from the Bear Clan Mother that allowed me to participate in and observe the crossover rituals that follow. It also considers the cultural context, grapples with the methodology, and explores the work that Iakoiane Wakerahkats:teh hoped to achieve in healing the nation. Next, in chapter 2, the text considers the creation story of the Haudenosaunee (Iroquois) and the Three Sisters story of sustaining Creation. In this chapter, we ponder how the Clan Mother retrieves the ancestral wisdom found in the Creation narrative and interprets it for contemporary practice. The third chapter examines the roles, duties, and responsibilities of the Bear Clan Mother as formulated by the Great Law. Chapter 4 reviews the life stages of Haudenosaunee girls and boys as they become initiated into adulthood and full participation within the community. This chapter considers the importance of ritual as the community invites, initiates, and sustains the rebuilding of a nation. Then the chapter examines in detail two Crossover Ritual initiation rites. Chapter 5 highlights global issues related to indigenous social movements with particular focus on key concerns over land, water, and human rights. Finally, the book reiterates the importance of the work of this Bear Clan Mother in her desire to retrieve the ancient wisdom of her people for contemporary times and the resilience of the people.

I am very grateful for Iakoiane Wakerahkats:teh's willingness to share the cultural memory of her people. Throughout the text, Iakoiane Wakerahkats:teh expounds vital information based upon oral history of the Haudenosaunee and contemporary cultural practices. Her longer passages will be formatted into extracts so that the reader may easily identify her voice as separate from my own.

The Call of the Earth Mother

> Inside the medicine of time there is one certain truth: that life upon this earth is always in a constant chasm of renewal. So, whether by choice or by calamity, life as we know it is on the cusp of a colossal upheaving. Delivered through prayers inside the womb of a moon lodge, the Earth Mother speaks and I am reminded of my stewardship and my duty to women.
>
> My indigenous grandmothers stood upon the ocean cliffs when the first wave of European saltwater men hit the shores of our sacred Turtle Island. For twenty-one thousand moons my people have watched their adolescent behavior wreak havoc across our beautiful and pristine earth. In my peoples' language, we call her Ieti'nisten:ha Ohon:tsa.[32] In times of mindless play and risky behaviors, we sat and shared our wisdom about being too wasteful, our leaders warned saltwater men to tread lightly in her presence. Saltwater men mocked the words of the Noble Red Men.
>
> Now that saltwater man is maturing, he is beginning to reflect upon his selfish choices. Earth Mother has been patient, as all mothers are. The time has come for her to correct his behavior; in stern warnings we hear her voice across the land as environmental casualties take place around the earth. Clearly she is saying, "Clean up your mess, my salt water son."
>
> In gentle echoes across vast mountaintops Ieti'nisten:ha Ohon:tsa calls forward her saltwater son:
>
> "Come here my son, stand in front of me, come closer, hang your head and place your ear upon my heart. Hear it beating, hear the many prayers I have prayed for you, taste the

tears that fell from my eyes when I feared for you, touch the scars where my heart broke for you, smell the blood that gave life to you. Close your eyes and see the sacred door through which you entered your life and know that no matter what you have done, my heart still loves you.

"Lift your head, gaze into the eyes of your Earth Mother and tell me that you're ready to make your amends. Throw your arms around me and say you're sorry for the pain that you have caused me. Be humble in your request. Throw out your masculine ego, your greed, and your self-serving agenda. Fall upon your knees in front of me and ask for my pity. Even the wild beast of the forest knows how to humble himself in the presence of an Earth Mother, for I am the very breath that all living things breathe.

"My saltwater son, I prepare you for your condolence. I remove from you the burden of your choices. I wipe away your tears with the softness of a fawn's hide, so that you can see clearly my beauty; with an eagle feather I remove the dust from your ears so you can hear the wisdom in my words, my son with the life-giving power from the springs of the earth I give sacred water to you, drink, clear your throat so you can now speak as a man with honor. There is no more time for foolish play. I give you instructions: Without haste go to all corners of the earth and echo this call. I bestow upon you a duty to carry a message from your Earth Mother. Call all indigenous mothers of the earth—past, present, and future—to a land of convergence. A land that still runs clear with sweet water from the mountain tops, a land that still holds my pristine beauty. It is here that mothers and grandmothers of the earth will usher in a time of tremendous earthly renewal. It has always been your job to honor and protect women. That is why I gave you strength—go quickly for you cannot fail in the delivery of my calling; if you do, the heart of your mother, will stop beating."

We have to reindiginate our earth because everyone of this earth is indigenous, part of an original seed that grew from her, our Earth Mother. All women embody the earth; through all women, Mother Earth speaks. It is now time for rematriation,[33] children of the earth! The time has come to return ourselves to the place of Mother.

1

Setting the Context

> There is no power for change greater than a community discovering what it cares about.
>
> —Margaret J. Wheatley

The title of this book is a deliberate double entendre. It refers at once to Clan Mother's sense of calling, that is, to her life experience, her "spiritual journey" toward self-discovery and assuming her role as Clan Mother. It also refers to the call that Clan Mother extends to her people, that is, to her own voice and to the content of her teaching. Since in so many ways Clan Mother is what she teaches and teaches what she is, my text integrates relevant biographical material in tandem with the narratives and rituals that Clan Mother shares and presides over. My hope is that her biography and teachings will continually illuminate each other, much as they did in the real-life encounters that produced the material for this book. This is the format in which the Clan Mother herself was most comfortable.

This chapter provides the context out of which this research was conducted. First, it considers issues related to culture. While the chapter includes discussion of the methodology that I integrated in producing the book, it secondarily focuses on how Bear Clan Mother seeks to retrieve, reclaim, and reconstruct the cultural memory of her people.

The reproduction of cultural survival is both a biological and an ideological construction. Research in collective memory and historical identity recognizes that critical to obtaining one's cultural identity and assuming survival are language, ceremonial practices, and the maintenance of principles regarding everyday life.[1] One element that continually emerges in the rebuilding of a people is the need to maintain and transmit the language that carries their intimate and complex worldview. I was moved by Iakoiane Wakerahkats:teh's remarks on this subject:

> The vision to lead our youth into a place of wellness through a regeneration of our culture could not be met with incredible reward if it did not embrace our own language. Kaniekeh:ha, my native language, a gift from my mother who did not speak English, showered me in the sweet melody of a mother tongue in my growing years. Native language, in its purest form, is the key to open the celestial door to ancestral knowledge as we begin to help our young in a monumental crossover as they journey to seek the meaning of their lives.[2]

In my book *Cultural Memory: Resistance, Faith and Identity*, coauthored with cultural anthropologist Dr. Ted Fortier, we constructed a theoretical framework for engaging cultural memory. Our intent was to explore this phenomenon by isolating and analyzing the content, transmission, and sources of empowerment. This included the selection and passage of memories from generation to generation. We examined the construct of this theoretical framework by looking at elements of cultural memory as evidenced within different communities, and through doing so identified six distinct elements of cultural memory: identity, reconstruction, enculturation, transmission, obligations, and reflexivity.[3]

Our intent was not to undertake a definitive, comparative analysis, but rather to explore the ways in which these practices sustained collective beliefs, maintained cultural distinctiveness, and stimulated dignity and defiance in the face of injustice. Now, at Bear Clan Mother's invitation, and with her collaboration, I will utilize the fruits of that research on understanding cultural memory in order to elevate the voice of a contemporary Clan Mother (Kanien'kehá:ka) of the Haudenosaunee (Iroquois[4]), who seeks to retrieve, reclaim, and transmit the cultural memory of her people. Native American scholar José Barreiro offers us a detailed description of the duties of Clan Mothers:

> She must perpetuate the ways of our people; she must be able to teach the ways of our people to the young people. She must be able to look out for large amounts of people because now, all of the clan people are family. And so, because of the changing of the times, in these days we don't necessarily

> have the eldest women being Bear Clan Mother of certain clans, but the eldest eligible woman. We cannot have someone teaching our children our traditional ways who does not follow the traditional ways themselves and cannot perpetuate this way. Some have followed a foreign way, maybe they have become Christianized, or maybe they are following, let's say the government of another country, the United States. They cannot be truly one of our people because once a person begins following another way of thinking, their thoughts cannot be pure and clean anymore, totally for the people, for the good of perpetuating the traditions which are so important among our people.[5]

The power of cultural memory rests in the conscious decision to choose particular memories and to give those memories precedents within communal memories. Literature review, archival work, and oral history will all be important pieces for this work, for how we remember the past has a profound impact on our actions and the way by which we lead our lives, as well as how we relate to other communities.

It is important to incorporate a number of methods in this kind of work. The principle method I ground myself in is what Eduardo Duran defines as liberation discourse. That is, speaking in a voice that is decolonized or at least in a process of being decolonized, "allowing the once-colonized to reinvent themselves in a manner that is within their control."[6] Clan Mother Iakoiane Wakerahkats:teh prefers to contend that her people are reindigenizing themselves, and in fact the Haudenosaunee "never surrendered to the colonizer."[7] Researchers tell us that systems of recovery and the promotion of indigenous knowledge are important processes in decolonizing indigenous nations.

> Recovering and maintaining indigenous world views, philosophies, and ways of knowing and applying those teachings in a contemporary context represents a web of liberation strategies indigenous people can employ to disentangle themselves from the oppressive control of colonizing state governments.[8]

Numerous scholars in multiple fields (e.g., theology, anthropology, history, politics, etc.) have explored the effects of the conquest on indigenous people. In addition to deaths caused by warfare, forced labor, brutality, and subjugation, many native people died from endemic diseases. Those that survived adjusted to the multitude of circumstances in which they found themselves. They had to adapt and perhaps change many of their customs, values, and beliefs. And yet, among them remained the ancient ones, the teachers, the loved ones, the women, who maintained a seed of the original instruction, which was passed down from generation to generation. The Crossover Rituals became the entry points of knowledge and understanding of life and creation. They create a map for reawakening one's personal and planetary position in the universe. And so, when Iakoiane Wakerahkats:teh reports to me that her people are reindigenizing themselves, what she is referring to is that despite her people's personal and generational experiences of trauma, "the fragmented pieces still contain our spirit."[9] The preceding comments on healing[10] are certainly appropriate for pre-contact culture.

However, the processes of revitalization that the Bear Clan Mother employs are directed at a reinterpretation of the tradition for contemporary young women. In a socio-centric culture such as the Haudenosaunee, the importance of bridging the ego-centered Western constructions with the ideology of the nation in its best formulation is seen in the symbol of the Moon Lodge, and how that ancient symbol is understood today. The type of healing employed by Iakoiane Wakerahkats:teh is not limited to an individual self, but is applicable to the context of cultural healing as well.

While it is difficult to generalize Native American beliefs and experiences because each community has its own unique identity, history, and response to the world, indigenous communities do have some shared memories that connect them to one another and to their ancestors. In a sense, one can still see their footprints on this earth: they laid out the path to guide others. It is the shared memory of why one walks the same path of life that they did, and this path is referred to as "original instruction."[11]

Original instruction entails a movement away from Western Cartesian thinking, which alienates people from the natural world, making the natural world an object that can be perceived and "managed" as separate from one's immediate existence. This book attempts to bridge these separate worldviews, so that indigenous peoples and Western Europeans might reclaim who they are and to whom they belong, questions that are at the core of identity and belonging.

Over successive generations, First Nation people from around the globe have experienced the trauma of colonization and marginalization: "For hundreds of years, North America's colonizers worked systematically to eradicate the indigenous cultural practices, religious beliefs, and autonomous political systems many among us now venerate."[12] Despite these efforts, indigenous peoples have survived. Sadly, while there exists extensive literature that documents these assaults,[13] few record indigenous resilience or their desire to retrieve, reclaim, and nurture a still-living culture.

As indigenous communities around the world are gathering to both reclaim and share their ancestral wisdom, cultural contact, cultural change, and cultural adaptations are a given. Environments shift, new information arrives, foreign concepts and material goods travel continually across borders. No culture can remain static and survive over the centuries; rather, cultures devise strategies to understand new elements and connect their core values with the wisdom of their respective pasts.

Haudenosaunee and First Nation communities, who once spanned the territory from Lake Ontario to the mouth of the St. Lawrence River, are now diminished in size. Yet they are still large in the reach of their extended families residing on either side of the US-Canadian border. These connections of families and extended families transcend political and territorial barriers, for the Native Americans are connected not only to their immediate and extended family but "also to all the generations that have walked upon the land and to the unborn faces yet to come."[14] This is largely because the Haudenosaunee, who refer to themselves as "the people of the longhouse," believe that they share kinship with all who reside on Turtle Island.

Many kinds of memories, specifically historical memories, are transmitted orally as well as through text, history, symbols, tradition, place, dreams, and narratives. What is significant for this work specifically is that the Haudenosaunee are highly oral in their tradition. The insights of Herbert Hirsch are useful in understanding this:

> In attempting to reconstruct our own history from what Langer (1991) calls the "ruins of memory" we should be aware of the fact that what we come up with is composed partially of remembered experiences, partially of events that we have heard about that may be part of a family or group mythology, partially of images that we have recreated from a series of family remembered events . . . historians and philosophers agree that personal recollections are used to formulate both the individual and the collective past . . . it is an attempt to chronicle human events remembered by human beings. History is moved by a series of social forces, including economics, religion, and institutions, mainly political, technological, ideological, and military.[15]

Just as historians create memory as they write history, this text documents a lived tradition and consequently creates an opportunity to explore another way of reconstructing memory.

Throughout this book, I will observe and document (as much as I have been given permission to) the call and original instructions transmitted by Iakoiane Wakerahkats:teh. These instructions, Chief Jake Swamp tells us,

> have become our shared memories about how humans are to conduct ourselves on this land we called North America. The instructions provide us frames of reference for looking at our relationship with the sacred universe, our first extended family. . . . We are connected to a great web of life.[16]

Iakoiane Wakerahkats:teh echoes and reaffirms this message through her own work as a Grandmother Moon ceremonialist. In her role as Bear Clan Mother and Lead Matron of the Moon Lodge Society, she underscores the need to reclaim their Crossover Ceremonies, because it is these rites that give indigenous youth a sense of purpose, dignity, and belonging. Connecting the people and celebrating the most important changes in their lives with them give the young adults this meaning. Crossover Ceremonies are young peoples' entry into ancient knowledge and a timeless understanding of life. The life changes they pass through as well as their own personal stories are connected with and given meaning through the larger creation story.

> [The] clan Mother's duties have to do with the community affairs, the nation affairs, but they also have another role and that has to do with the spiritual side. . . . they must perpetuate the [traditional] ways but they must also set ceremonial times and be able to watch the moon for our people. We don't have many people in this time who can communicate with the stars. . . . She must watch and always be ready to call the people together.[17]

She is also quick to contend that her people have experienced not just individual trauma but intergenerational trauma that continues to affect their lives today, the core of their spirit. These traumas then, are things that cannot be minimized or compared with others. Iakoiane Wakerahkats:teh states:

> Any time the soul experiences trauma, whether in its mother's womb, as a baby, a child, an adolescent teenager, a young

> adult, a middle-aged adult, an elder, pieces of our spirit and its essence become shattered. The fragmented pieces however still contain our spirit, and so to heal from the emotional pain caused by these traumatic events, these broken shards must be collected and attended to. All traumatic experiences that are unattended, unprocessed, or untreated result in loss.[18]

Ultimately, this loss not only impacts the individual but the whole community, as traumatic experiences link generation to generation in a damaging cycle.

This book is, first of all, for the empowerment of women and youth, as well as native people who desire to learn more about their culture and practices as articulated by Clan Mother Iakoiane Wakerahkats:teh. For the reader who is not Native American, any vestiges of a reductive, rationalistic view of the world will be challenged by other epistemological postures. Those in the helping professions within these marginalized and misunderstood communities will recognize individuals and communities within the historical and current context that native peoples experience, and with it the legacy of generational trauma and resilience.

2

The Epoch of Sky Woman

Spiritualism is the highest form of political consciousness.

—"Haudenosaunee Address to the Western World"

In her work to retrieve ancestral wisdom, the Bear Clan Mother offers a version of the Haudenosaunee (Iroquois) Creation story that both grounds the people in an identity and calls them to participate within their community. This chapter considers that creation story in tandem with the Three Sisters story of sustaining Creation.

In one's assumptive world, culture concept is an integral element and plays a crucial role in how one understands who they are and to whom they belong. Within the pages of this book, culture is understood as "socially transmitted, often symbolic, information that shapes human behavior and regulates human society so that people can successfully maintain themselves and reproduce. Culture has mental, behavioral, and material aspects; it is patterned and provides a model for proper behavior."[1]

Therefore, to appreciate another person, one must appreciate his or her assumptive world or psychosocial reality. The process of enculturation posits a worldview as a fact and connects the variety of experiences into a creation that constitutes their individual reality; it is out of this reality that all rationality flows: "Haudenosaunee see history as Epochal. We are currently in the Third Epoch of Time. Earth's history began in the First Epoch [with] Haudenosaunee time center[ing] around the great spiritual events of each Epoch."[2]

How we remember past events has a profound impact on what we do and how we live. While personal memory is the cornerstone supporting both collective and social memory, memory cannot be fully understood as separate from social forces. One way memory is transmitted is through narrative, which emphasizes the active, self-shaping quality of human thought. Its power resides in its ability to recreate, refashion, and reclaim identity: it is this power that Iakoiane Wakerahkats:teh is calling forth. The first step of the process to reclaim and sustain one's identity and to ground oneself is to understand one's Story of Origin.

Before we delve into the Haudenosaunee's Creation Story of Origin, I offer few words about tradition and tales. For these insights, I am grateful to the research conducted by Barbara Alice Mann and present her understanding of the terms "traditional" and "keepings."

The Creation Story

Iroquoian "keepings," or traditions, come in four major varieties. There are the "truly tales," or historically accurate stories, which are often told through the aid of a wampum belt, a form of writing for the Haudenosaunee. The word "wampum" means white shell beads, which were originally used as a medium to console oneself in grief. Later, wampum belts were made to record and recognize agreements made with the Europeans.[3] The second form of Haudenosaunee narrative can be found in "walking tales," in which the keeper, or oral traditionalist, begins with the words "See the man walking," or "It is as if that man is walking." This phrase indicates that the story about to be told is fictional. While differentiated by their varying relationships to historical accuracy, truly and walking tales both "deal in mundane matters and lack a cosmic focus."[4] A third variety of narrative is what is known as the spirit stories. They often begin with "That woman went to the field," or "That man went to the pond." These stories are very popular, but "regardless of how the story session begins it is likely to end with telling and retellings of ghostly beginnings."[5] Finally, there are the traditional tales, which are narratives that have very strong spiritual meanings that traditional Iroquois regard as factual. They are the lynchpins of memory, basic to the spiritual experience that is Iroquoian reality. Tales in all of these genres contain what folklorists and anthropologists call learning stories, or " 'sophisticated analogies that make deliberate and conscious points about social principles, religious beliefs, and cultural values.' "[6] This research is helpful in understanding the varieties of stories of origin and aiding the acceptance of Haudenosaunee epistemology. This is because "morality inherently provides room for flexibility and outright change . . . outreach[ing] the Western notion that there is only one right version of ancient texts."[7] The keepers, or oral traditionalists, argue in great latitude over how one tells the story and how "particular keepers will be recognized by consensus as providing better or weaker versions, yet, even that consensus version is liable to change from time to time, from nation to nation—and from women to men."[8]

Creation myths and stories of origin have a symbolic meaning within specific cultures and describe peoples' earliest beginnings. The Christian approach as influenced by Greek philosophy projects Creation as something outside the Creator. Humans stand outside material creation and wield the power to dominate and exploit, whereas the Native American approach to Creation champions one's relationship with Mother Earth as reciprocal. The interpretation of cultural ideas from the indigenous language into English is always difficult. How does one really convey their richness of symbolic realities into another system, which does not share these ideals? As the author, I try to use cognates that have some sense of the original idea and develop conceptualization along those lines. The history of missions, and the degradation of native spirituality, has been well documented: the use of the term Creator is common among Indian nations today, and, alternately using a non-English term serves both to mark the idea and to reflect the processes of enculturation and accommodation.

Indigenous ancestors carried an incredible amount of knowledge that was gathered through their experience of the land and every living being. They understood that part of being human was to be grateful for everyday life, so they nurtured and respected nature as its own entity. The path of the Original Instructions articulated by the Haudenosaunee is echoed in the Earth Charter of 1987. Jake Swamp, a member of the Haudenosaunee, has articulated that the

> relationships between people, cultures, and even nations are predicated upon three simple values. The first is to love each other as if we were one large extended family. The second says that we are meant to share with one another. Third, humans have been asked to respect the life's breath that enters our bodies that allows us to exist.[9]

There are different versions of how the world began, but the purpose of this book is to document how one contemporary Clan Mother transmits ancient teachings to the next generation. What follows, then, is how this particular Clan Mother of the Kanien'kehá:ka nation articulates and transmits the Creation Story in her own words. The understanding of this origin story is significant and reenacted in the Crossover Rituals described in chapter 3.

While there are a number of versions of any creation story, this particular creation story has basic components that convey core cultural values: that the immortal time for the Haudenosaunee begins in Sky World above this Earth, that there are spiritual beings who make their home on this earth, and that the protagonists of the story are Iottsi'tsi:son (Sky Woman)[10] and (Sky Chief). As the story unfolds, Sky Woman (also referenced as Mature Flower), falls from the Sky World while pregnant. It is important to understand that, at this time, there is no Earth—when Sky Woman descends from Sky World, she is falling into what is considered a "primal sea."[11] As she is falling, Canada geese interlock their wings and break her fall, helping her land on the top of a great turtle. The narrative continues by describing the collaboration of Sky Woman and the animals in constructing the land.

Upon Sky Woman's landing, the gathered animals begin to dive to the bottom of the ocean to gather and retrieve dirt. The beaver, the otter, the pickerel, each tries and not only fails but dies in his attempt to retrieve the precious earth. At last, the muskrat manages to grab some of the muck in his paw but dies when he surfaces from the exhausting and heroic task. Using the fruits of his sacrifice, Sky Woman sings, dances, and pats the muck on the turtle's back. As she dances, the turtle and muck begin to expand. This becomes the pivotal point of the creation of the Earth: the earth that Sky Woman magically created on that day has since been known as "Mother Earth." Because Mother Earth is atop this great turtle, Sky Woman gave the name Turtle Island to this land, which is the reason why many First Nations people refer to North America as Turtle Island.

Sky Woman then has a daughter, Iakotsitsio:te (which means Standing Flower),[12] who later gives birth to twin boys, Tahroniawa:kon (Sky Holder) and Sawiskaron (Flint). Unlike the Judaic Creation Story that focuses on one omnipresent God who creates the world, the Haudenosaunee's cosmological transformation of the world involves not only a complex series of events but a series of beings.

Out of the several stories in their tradition, let us hear one of Iakoiane Wakerahkats:teh's versions in her own words. Mindful that there are other substantive versions such as John Mohawk's 2005 Iroquois Creation Story[13] and the beautiful narrative offered by Tom Porter in "And Grandma Said . . . ,"[14] what follows is Clan Mother Wakerahkats:teh's personal retelling:[15]

The story begins in a place we call Ionnehon:we, the alive, original place. Rote;seron;kies (Lightning Bolt) was an uncle to a boy and a girl (Sky Woman), both children of destiny, who lived at the edge of a village in Sky World.

Lightning Bolt puts his niece and nephew under vigilant guard, shrouded under cattails and corn husk in a place of concealment. He keeps the children away from the main village and takes charge of raising them alongside their mother. After some time, Lightning Bolt dies. After his passing, he appears to his niece in a dream world, to console and instruct her of her purpose.

In a world of isolation with only her mother and brother in existence, Sky Woman grew into her adolescence with a deep loneliness for her uncle, often finding herself visiting the place of his burial. Within a dream, Lightning Bolt foretells that the big chief in the main village, Rarontanon:na (Sky Chief), caretaker of the Life Tree that bears all seeds and fruits, would one day send for her. Lightning Bolt instructs her to answer Sky Chief's call when the time comes, encouraging her to listen to what Sky Chief would instruct her to do. Lightning Bolt further tells her that Sky Chief would present a dowry for her hand in marriage to her mother. Although Sky Woman did not want this to happen, she respected the words of her uncle.

News of Lightning Bolt's death and of his sister's isolated family caught Sky Chief's attention. Intrigued, Sky Chief sent a messenger to get Sky Woman's mother to escort Sky Woman to his lodge so that they could speak. He told her of a dream he wished to have interpreted, which nobody in the village could understand. The fact that nobody could understand its meaning made Sky Chief very troubled. He knew of Sky Woman, he knew of her extreme beauty and her ability to talk to spirits. This was why he had asked that she be brought to his lodge to interpret his dream. As foretold by her deceased uncle, Sky Chief offered a dowry to the mother for her daughter's hand in marriage in exchange for her uncanny ability. Sky Woman's mother accepted, and so when the day came and Sky Chief called her into his presence, she went. She was sixteen years old at the time.

Upon entering the village, Sky Woman cast her eyes upon other people for the first time. She walked past a field of many men playing a brutal game with a stick and a ball, with her shyness keeping her eyes in a downward glance. With little introduction at the door of Sky Chief's stately lodge, he immediately gave her a task. Amid his incredible wealth and power, he had ordered that a grand feast take place in honor of her arrival. However, it was her duty to prepare the ceremonial food of corn mush. This meant she had to fetch water to fill the big clay pot he had arranged for her, as a test of her loyalty. Sky Chief motioned her toward a long path that led to the river and with strict voice told her not to talk to anyone on her journey. He stated that her focus was needed to have the corn mush made in a timely fashion.

On her first trip to the river a wolf approached her, which she ignored and walked past. She returned with the vessel full of water to fill the pot. Then she visited the river a second time, and a bear approached her. Again, she refused to acknowledge this character, as each time the animal character came in a manly form. Without a glance, Sky Woman refused each of these men. After every rejection, they would shape-shift back into their original animal form and run back into the woods. On her third trip returning from the river she was hurrying down the path that ran along the field where the intense medicine game of lacrosse was being played to uplift the troubled mind of Sky Chief.

In the scuffle of the game, the ball was thrown toward her, and in a swift motion a lacrosse player with great speed caught the ball before it hit her. In his speedy retrieval of the ball, he gently brushed her hand holding the pot.

This moment when Sky Woman meets the lacrosse player is paramount, but many storytellers leave it out and ignore its significance. This is where the story needs to be rematriated. Because it is here where the magic happens that brings this story to a significant truth. So, through the lens of a feminine heart I know without a doubt that this is where all women began to recognize their inner knowing. So, whether it was centuries ago in the Sky World or it was yesterday alongside a lacrosse field, there is an undeniable truth known as "the law of attraction."

It is in this moment of near collision that Sky Woman was jolted from her concentration on her mission. For the first time in her young life, she looked into the face of a handsome young man. His eyes presented her with new possibilities. In a moment beyond her control, the young lacrosse player leaned close to her and with a boyish smile asked if he could quench his thirst with a drink of water from her clay pot. Sky Woman shyly took pity upon his need and let him drink the cool water. As the lacrosse player drank from the rim of her clay pot, his eyes captured hers in a willful utterance that pierced her soul. Locked in a steadfast stare she melted into the power of his masculinity and he into her innocent beauty. Sky Woman began to feel things she never felt before, and all that is woman inside her emerged with a feminine force that burst her heart wide open. She was no longer lonely.

Call me a romantic but I know that our Creation Story is really a story of re-Creation, a love story of immense passion. Without it, the story is mundane and mechanical. Throughout the medicine of time there remains a colossal truth, and that is there is no feeling greater than that magical moment when two wandering souls connect.

The laughter of the other lacrosse players brought the lacrosse player and Sky Woman back to their original purposes. It was then that she realized she couldn't return to cook the mush with a half empty pot, so she returned to the river to refill it. By the time she got back to her cooking pot, Sky Chief had already heard the ripples of gossip that she had disobeyed him and was furious.

He had instructed her not to speak to anyone. As punishment for her disobedience, Sky Chief made her stand in front of the hot pot so that as she cooked near the hot flames, the mush splattered and burnt her skin. She did not flinch from the burns or complain, continuing to fulfill her duty. She took ownership of her unforeseen circumstance and remembered her uncle's instructions. After completing her task, Sky Chief had the dogs in the village lick her wounds. The dogs' salvia healed her burns, but she was scarred.

Sky Chief could not forgive her disloyalty so he told her to return to her mother's lodge. The mother upon hearing of what happened quickly weaved a basket and filled it with a deer hide for Sky Chief in hopes of returning honor to her daughter and to fulfill the dowry. Yet Sky Woman did not want to marry the old Sky Chief, so when her mother left to repay the dowry to Sky Chief, Sky Woman ran to gather the men in the village to uproot the Life Tree, of which Sky Chief was the protector.

Sky Chief was quickly told of the incident and hastened to the tree. Upon his arrival, he saw his bride to be standing at the edge of the celestial opening, staring down into a dark chasm. Standing in disbelief, the Sky Chief sees the Life Tree that he had been protecting was uprooted and quickly wilting. In the ferocity of his rage, Sky World shook, causing Sky Woman to lose her footing and fall through the dark chasm. Some storytellers say he pushed her; others say that he cast her out along with the lacrosse player. In any event, Sky Woman already knew that this would come to pass because of her uncle's prophecy, and the moment fulfilled the meaning of Sky Chief's dream. What a lot of people aren't aware of is that Sky Woman was not pregnant when she fell but arrived on earth pregnant.

It is easy for one to assume that she was pregnant with Sky Chief's baby. A lot of the old literature will say that, but when I recount this story as a woman who experienced a woman's first stirrings, I can easily recognize that the father of her baby was really the young lacrosse player. Many forget what happens during her fall out of the Sky World and who streaks across the sky to save her. As she fell out of Sky World, she grabbed on to what she could from the tangled roots of the Life Tree and its seeds got caught beneath her fingernails.

As she fell into the deep abyss, it is said that lacrosse player became a meteorite. Rohaserakeh:te (he carries light) streaked across the cosmos to catch her in her sudden fall. He carried her across the galaxy in his arms, protecting her, and shared with her provisions of corn and dried meat. It is during the fall that their relationship became intimate. But once she came into the Earth's gravitational pull, he went ahead of her, penetrating the Earth's protective layer. As he disintegrated, his stardust enveloped her into a state of fertilization and procreation. It is in this regenerative explosion that conception occurs. Modern medical science concurs that human conception occurs with the fall of eggs into the fallopian tube. Sky Woman began to fall freely into the pull of the earth, which is when the geese saw her falling. Flying in a V formation, they flew to catch her, breaking her fall, and gently placed her on the shell of a sea turtle.

After that happens, pretty much the rest of the story is the same as the other versions except for the muskrat. The muskrat was the one able to retrieve the earth from the ocean floor to put on the turtle's back, and when she danced, pregnant, the earth grew rapidly. She danced counterclockwise and gave birth to her daughter. Her daughter's name is Iakotsitsio:te, which means "she has a flower on her."

The daughter grew quickly and when the daughter grew into her adolescence, she started to realize how lonely she was because it was only her and her mother on the Earth. She would go out and play and create imaginary friends. Then finally, raccoon showed up and asked her for her hand in marriage. She replied that she was uncertain and had best go back to ask her mother. So, she went and asked her mother, who decided he couldn't have her hand in marriage. The next time she met a sly fox that asked for her hand in marriage. Again, she said she needed her mother's permission. And again, Sky Woman refused the company of the fox for her daughter. Finally, the third character appears. Rohontsiawakon (he holds the earth) the Turtle showed up, muddy and ungroomed, and wasn't charming like the first two suitors. Again, she said she would have to ask her mother.

This time, Sky Woman agreed to meet her daughter's suitor. Once she had accepted the meeting, Turtle Man gave her instructions: "I will arrive at your lodge at dusk. Prepare me a meal." When her daughter returned, she and Sky Woman prepared a meal for his arrival. He arrived, ate his meal, and shortly after dusk Turtle Man and the Sky Woman agreed upon his marriage to her daughter. Under a stormy and starry night sky, Turtle Man and Iakotsitsio:te laid down feet to feet in an east and west direction. Turtle Man placed two arrows on her abdomen, and that is when she conceived twins by the symbol of two arrows. This act of conception brought cosmic order, centering the axis of the earth, aligning the turbulent winds and oceans currents in a counterclockwise rotation of the earth's spin. Turtle Man was the only suitor that could engineer this colossal feat. Without him the first earthly conception could not have occurred. Yet even before the first rays of light, Turtle Man left his young bride, never to be seen again. Abandonment is a repetitive theme throughout this story. However, the impending birth did not leave the two women in self-pity for too long and both got to the task at hand.

Immediately after conception and upon the symbol of the two arrows it became apparent that twins were developing in the womb of Iakotsitsio:te. The two cosmic wholes started to compete with each other inside their mother. Iakotsitsio:te struggled to maintain a safe environment for her developing twin boys. Both had tremendous power and with each passing stage she labored more to maintain a balance between the two. In the gush of birth the more robust twin was first to ready himself to be born in natural course. His twin brother became jealous and decided he didn't want to be born second. He had sharp bones on his body from a deformity, so he cut his way out of his mother's body through her armpit, wanting to do the opposite of his brother. Sadly, Iakotsitsio:te, daughter of Sky Woman, died in childbirth.

The dynamics between the twin brothers is very interesting. Sky Woman, now a grandmother, named her twin grandsons. She named one born grandson Tahronhiawa':kon, which means Sky Holder, and the second grandson Sawiskara, or Flint. Sawiskara was so named because shortly after their birth, their mother's body became cold as flint. It is said that Sky Holder, the more benevolent brother, tried to enhance humanity whereas his brother Flint was inclined to do the opposite and make things difficult for the human race. Yet, it is the brothers' duality that is a complementary concept that keeps the world in balance. Hence, balance is a high priority on the scale of values for us Haudenosaunee. It is these cosmic twinned wholes that represents the duality in the human experience. However, it is important to recognize that without Iakotsitsio:te, the twins would have no entry and the Earth no balance.

The twins grew rapidly. Sky Holder and Flint loved their mother. Each became lonely for her love and would return to the place of her death. Using his sharp bones, Flint severed his mother's head and placed it on a pole outside the grandmother's lodge so that he could see her every day. When Sky Holder returned to see her and found her head missing, he followed the trail of blood that led him to the lodge of his twin brother and grandmother. He saw what Flint had done and became angry. Drowned in grief, he took his mother's head and flung it into the sky, allowing her beautiful face to shine down brightly against the backdrop of the night.

In this moment, we recognize that she became the moon and we understand why a total lunar eclipse is called a blood moon. Sky Holder gave her a dress made of stars to magnify her beauty. In continual honor he gave her purpose: for all time to come, she would lead the women on Earth. Her duty was to guide the future generations that would grow from the earth. He gave her tremendous power to control the tides of the oceans, and the currents of the rivers, and all the water veins of the earth were under her power. She also had the power to pull forth the life from the gardens. Her path was to follow the dance of her Mother Sky Woman counterclockwise around the Earth, so she too circles the Earth in a trailing motion. And so, to this very day, the women in the longhouse dance the same way. Sky Woman and her daughter danced for life, in a feminine relationship to the Earth. Iakotsitsio:te the moon was to bring light into the darkness of her son Flint. Sky Holder gave his mother an honorable position in the Creation Story and placed her at a center point in the universe. Because of her position in the planetary alignments, she is Earth's protector and shield, deflecting the meteorites that enter her gravitational pull. Her position entailed great responsibility, and once Sky Holder was done honoring his late mother, he decreed that for all time she would be the leader of all women. It is also said that meteorite showers are the lacrosse player showering his love every now and again to his Sky Woman and their daughter, the moon.

Then Sky Holder and Flint continued to make creations, each adding his own expression to their creations.

Every time Sky Holder created something beautiful like the rose, his brother Flint would put thorns on it. The great duality of life begins with these twins. It wasn't so much that one was good and one was evil, but that one brother was jealous of the other because the one brother was born strong and healthy and the other was born with an abnormality.

The grandmother, Sky Woman, favored the deformed, sick one. When the twin brothers became young men, their grandmother gave them each an arrow that was a symbol of their conception. She gave Sky Holder the blunt, crooked arrow, while she gave the sick brother the strong arrow with a tip so he would be able to hunt and bring food to him and her. The reason that the grandmother resented Sky Holder was because the other brother, Flint, blamed him for the death of their mother.

Of course the grandmother was also grieving for the loss of her daughter and the fact that she had been left to raise her twin grandsons who were in constant conflict. She decides to let the strong one fend for himself, while she takes care of the weak one. When Sky Holder created, Flint tried to rip up his creations, and this is how the cosmic wholes began to compete for control of creation.

This great battle ensued throughout each piece of creation because Flint tried to be more powerful than Sky Holder. They got into a physical fight and it was the grandmother that had to intervene, and this is where she brought in a peach bowl game to settle the sibling rivalry. Sky Holder returned to those things in creation to help him in this great contest. In the end, Sky Holder outwitted his brother and won the game but, due to his compassionate nature, decided to divide the wealth of their creation, ushering in the time of the continental divide.

Sky Holder put everything his brother had created on the European and African continent and relegated his own creations on the North and South American continents. In between them he let the saltwater oceans flow. Sky Holder said to his twin brother, "I will rule the day and you will rule the night," allowing for a division of power. And so inside of us there is always that duality of the twins. It's about the constant inner struggle of humanity, about working hard or about taking the easy way out. Inside everyone exists these twins. Every day is a struggle about how you are going to approach life and how you choose to live the life given you.

For me, the Creation Story contains many themes but is mostly about how to find balance within the human experience. It is about how male and female complement each other in a world of re-creation. Sky Holder revered his mother, longed for his mother, and she was taken away from him. But, she became a powerful force within the creation story. It is Sky

Woman who is the bringer of the life that sustains our earth also became part of the earth.

As we move through life, we look to our creation story for guidance on how to conduct ourselves today. The story's lessons still hold true.

An earth man was created in this story and was given an earth woman as a partner. Woman in human form was the last of Sky Holder's creations. He molded an earth woman, his finest creation, a masterpiece in the image of his mother. In her abdomen he placed the perpetual seeds of humanity and centered her upon the earth as the bringer of life, placing her at the very thresholds of life and death. He connected her regenerative powers to the cycling of his mother the moon and that is why women bleed and renew themselves. Without Sky Woman and her daughter, we wouldn't have the coming generations to continue the breath of life.

There is more to the story but I will stop here.

~

The significance of reiterating the creation story in the voice of Iakoiane Wakerahkats:teh is that a review of literature on Native Americans reveals that many times the Haudenosaunee creation story is discussed and then interpreted through a Christian framework. For example, the interpretation of Sky Woman's two sons being opposing forces, that is, the dark one and the good one.[16] Clan Mother tells me that this is a specifically Christian perspective: that it's not about the forces of good and evil, but rather the significance of balance and harmony. As Mann wrote,

> The point of the Twins' tale is obviously the sacred role of cosmic equilibrium, a steady principle guiding most of the social inventions of the Iroquoian peoples. Among other things, equilibrium was the animating purpose behind "gendering," or the interaction between male and female energies that dictated the separation of social functions by gender. Like the Twins, the sexes functioned as cooperative halves.[17]

A distinctive point in this version of the Creation is that female figures hold a prominent place not only in the Creation Story but in the stories of Native People in general. They continue to influence modern-day Haudenosaunee society. Their creation stories have a direct correlation with women and their intimate relationship with land and her fruits. "Women don't have to see power in their traditions and ceremonies because they retain their power in the same way that the Corn Mother sustains her people. Woman's role is connected to food production, as well as to Mother Earth."[18] Native women also had great knowledge of herbs for culinary and medicinal purposes and were diplomats, politicians, and arbiters. "The Three Sisters" are an exemplary example of how the Haudenosaunee culture combines these concepts of women sustaining the people through their food production. The Three Sisters are a reference to the foundational, basic sustenance of the Haudenosaunee. In the Creation Story, Sky Woman falls from the Sky World with three types of seeds under her nails from the roots of the Life Tree: corn, beans, and squash. These seeds are now known as the Three Sisters and recognized as divine gifts. In returning to the land, contemporary Haudenosaunee restore the Three Sisters and, as a result of this process, strengthen all that they are.

Sustaining Creation (The Three Sisters)

Although Europeans used the technique of broadcasting their fields (scattering seeds haphazardly across plowed land), "Iroquoian women had learned the spirit secrets of seeds, however, and knew how deeply to bury each type; how much elbow room each needed to flower; the amount of sun each required; and how many seeds per dirt pocket insured plant growth."[19] This knowledge was evidenced in their planting organization:

> Sun-loving Sister Corn was planted on the mound tops . . . while every seventh mound, her shy Little Sister, Squash, lingered at the base, in the shadows, along with the clinging Little Sister, Bean, dotted around the base of her Elder Sister, Corn, onto whose limbs she might climb as she grew.[20]

The symbolism of the planting is also clearly apparent: "the intertwining arms of the Three Sisters, Daughters All of Mother Earth locked in a growing embrace, replicated the mutuality of their human counterparts, the female farmers supporting and sheltering one another according to the needs and strengths of each."[21] Even more symbolism can be gathered in alternative planting methods practiced by indigenous women:

> instead of planting beans at the base of the corn, the women would ring the entire field with bean vines. Low slinging

> limbs of trees edging the field would be staked to the ground, allowing Sister Bean to climb the symbolic male arms of protection, the natural palisades of the trees around the fields, creating a living wall of green protection encircling them.[22]

In Haudenosaunee agricultural economy, the Three Sisters demonstrate the important relationship of these life sustainers through the balance created in the nitrogen count of the soil. This section explored the power of narrative in sustaining creation through the retelling of Iakoiane Wakerahkats:teh's Creation Story, and with the help of the Three Sisters the next chapter will look at how this story of origin sustained the Haudenosaunee League. We will explore the League and the Great Law of Peace as important parts of the structure and identity of the Haudenosaunee with the Bear Clan Mother playing a significant part in the life of her people.

3

Clans and the Epoch of the League

Guided by the Eagle That Sees Afar.[1]

—Paul Wallace, *The Iroquois Book of Life: White Roots of Peace*

The Great Law of Peace serves as the constitution for the Haudenosaunee people. Its guiding principles call for unity and peace among the nations, prescribing their relationship with other human beings and all life. Yet perhaps the most identifiable characteristic of the Great Law is its recognition of the "status and suffrage accorded women by the Haudenosaunee [, with] approximately one-fourth of the Great Law's clauses recogniz[ing] the power and influence of women in the Iroquois culture."[2] This chapter presents the Haudenosaunee clans, as well as the roles, duties, and responsibilities of the Bear Clan Mother as formulated by the Great Law. The Great Law establishes "more than a code of conduct—it is also a beginning point for the modern clans. It embodies the foundations of all of the customs of holding meetings, of exchanging messages on wampums, and of assigning titles to leaders."[3]

Haudenosaunee Clans

Women are considered the progenitors of the Nation.

—"The Constitution of the Iroquois Nations:
The Great Binding Law, Gayanashagowa"

The Haudenosaunee (Iroquois Confederacy) is composed of six nations: the Kanien'kehá:ka (Mohawk), the Onayotekaono (Oneida), the Ononda'gega

(Onondaga), the Guyohkohnyoh (Cayuga), the Onondowahgah (Seneca), and the Ska-Ruh-Reh (Tuscarora). Each nation's societal structure is based on a system of clans that are composed of the progeny "of a woman and her female descendants."[4] Clan Mother Iakoiane Wakerahkats:teh refers to this hereditary process as a uterine line, underscoring the fact that the clan system is matrilineal, meaning that a person's clan is the same as his or her mother's clan. The clan system continues to exist today among the traditional Haudenosaunee. Most Haudenosaunee, whether of ancestral or of some other faith tradition, identify themselves as member of a particular clan, which is, in turn, headed by a Clan Mother. Only those individuals born to a Haudenosaunee mother with a clan have an undisputed right to Haudenosaunee citizenship. All Iroquoian women (gantowisas), specifically those in the role of Clan Mother, have duties that center upon matters of naming, identity, and citizenship. In fact, "the gantowisas enjo[y] sweeping political powers, which rang[e] from the administrative and legislative to the judicial. . . . They r[un] the funerals . . . appoint[t] warriors, declar[e] war, negotiate peace, and mediate disputes."[5]

> Women are indeed the first environment. . . . From the bodies of women flows the relationship of the generations both to society and the natural world. With our bodies we nourish, sustain, and create connected relationships and interdependence. In this way the Earth is our mother. In this way, we as women are the Earth.[6]

This also serves to cement the importance of women within the matrilineal Haudenosaunee society. As the individuals who bear children, the Haudenosaunee recognize that their community identity stems from their women. Women are finally integral to Haudenosaunee society in that they were also the first to recognize the message of the Peacemaker and the principles of the Great Law.

There are presently nine clans, each divided into animals from three earth elements: land, air, and water. The water creatures are comprised of the turtle, the beaver, and the eel; the land creatures include the deer, the wolf, and the bear; and the creatures of the sky consist of the hawk, the heron, and the snipe. The natural world is symbolized through the microcosm of these beings.

Faithkeepers acknowledge that prior to the Peacemaker, there were numerous other clans. According to the curator of the Iroquois Museum, after the formation of the confederacy, the number of clans was reduced to the nine represented in table 1.[8]

Table 1. Haudenosaunee Clans

Nation Name	Traditional Name	The People	The Animals
Mohawk	Kanien'kehá:ka	The People of Flint	Bear, Wolf, Turtle
Oneida	Onayotekaono	The People of the Standing Stone	Bear, Wolf, Turtle
Onondaga	Ononda'gega	The People of the Hills	Bear, Wolf, Turtle, Deer, Eel, Hawk, Beaver, Heron, Snipe
Cayuga	Guyohkohnyoh	The People of the Great Swamp	Bear, Wolf, Turtle, Heron, Snipe
Seneca	Onondowahgah	The People of the Great Hill	Bear, Wolf, Turtle, Beaver, Heron, Snipe, Hawk, Deer
Tuscarora	Ska-Ruh-Reh	The Shirt-Wearing People	Bear, Wolf, Turtle, Beaver, Snipe, Deer, Eel

The names of the clan come from the types of animals, but the clans themselves are arranged in moieties.

Haudenosaunee oral tradition speaks of a time when, due to increasing deaths within the population, the people found themselves in a state of unresolved grief. Many meetings were called, and after several discussions, a young man asked for permission to speak and told the people that they should "follow the example of nature which the Creator made. If the people followed the ways of nature, they too would divide themselves into manageable working groups."[8] Due to his stunning insight, the elders gave the young man a special name, Ronikonrowa:nan, or "he who has great ideas." This title remains in Haudenosaunee societal structure to this day.

Ronikonrowa:nan asked the people to follow him to the river. In the people's attempt to cross, the guiding vines broke, dividing the people on two banks. Ronikonrowa:nan told the women on his side that when morning came, they should pay attention to what they saw and give thanks to Sky Holder. The next morning, the eldest woman woke up, gave thanks to Sky Holder, and went down to the river to fetch water. Upon hearing a noise, she turned to see a deer standing at the bank of the river. When she returned to the others, Ronikonrowa:nan asked her if she had seen anything, and she replied that she had seen a deer by the water, and that the animal would be her clan. And so, the next day, another elderly woman took part in the same ritual and saw a bear. Again, she returned to the others, where Ronikonrowa:nan told her that "she and all [of] her offspring would from then on belong to the clan of the Bear."[9] So it happened that on the side of the river the people crossed, you have the Deer, Bear, Snipe, and Eel clans that would now always be united as a singular group.[10] The young man crossed the river again, returning to the opposite side where many of the families had been left behind. The ritual was then completed in the same way, so the people on the second side of the river received the Wolf, the Beaver, the Turtle, and the Hawk as their clan animals.[11]

As previously noted, the clans are named in accordance with various animal, bird, and fish life. Children born into this tradition assume their clans through their mothers, with this type of inheritance-based transmission known as a matrilineal system.

The symbol for the peace between the clans is a tree known as the Great Tree of Peace, whose roots are in Mother Earth. According to the Peacemaker, peace "flourished only in a garden amply fertilized with absolute and pure justice. It was the product of a spiritually conscious society using its abilities of reason that resulted in a healthy society."[12] However, before there was peace among the clans, the Haudenosaunee passed through a very dark period in their history, a time of brutality, conflict, division and war:

> The second epoch opens on the Iroquoian world at war. The insane Onondaga chief and shaman, Adodaroh, was terrorizing the people with his foreign-inspired cannibal cult, in a strong-man raiding society with its roots in the fading world of the hunt. Opposite the Cannibals stood the Cultivators, with their new crop-growing, woman-centered economy taking over as the primary means of sustenance.[13]

The Five Nations of the Seneca (comprised of the Mohawk, Onondaga, Oneida, Cayuga, and Seneca) forged the League of the Haudenosaunee in the area that is now known as New York State around AD 1000 to 1450. Later, the Tuscarora joined the League as the sixth nation in 1722. The Great Law of Peace that has been passed down from generation to generation governs all six nations. Still, other Iroquois, not all of them reservation or treaty people, live in Wisconsin, Oklahoma, Kansas, and Ontario, Canada.[14]

The narrative passed down is one involving a messenger sent from the Creator (the elders tell me that it is a custom of the people that his name would never be spoken outside of sharing the oral history in ceremony, and out of respect, I will simply refer to him as the Peacemaker[15]). All five nations tell the story of how this messenger was sent by Sky Holder to put an end to the warring of the five nations. It is said that the Peacemaker came from the Attiwendaronk, on the North Shore of Lake Ontario. He crossed the lake and approached the land of the Iroquois, driven forward by his task to "carry the mind of the Master of Life . . . and bring an end to the wars between East and West."[16] This peace, according to Paul Wallace, is that all people shall love one another and live in peace through the mediums of righteousness, health, and power, where "righteousness means justice . . . : it means also a desire to see justice prevail. Health means soundness of mind and body; . . . power means authority, the authority of law and custom . . . for justice enforced is the will of the Holder of the Heavens.' "[17] This peace, established through the aforementioned principles of justice,

> demand[s] that all thoughts of prejudice, privilege, or superiority be swept away, and that recognition is given to the reality that the creation is intended for the benefit of all equally—even the birds, animals, trees, and insects, as well as humans. The world does not belong to humans, it is the rightful property of the Creator.[18]

In light of this newly emergent worldview, the Peacemaker asked the Haudenosaunee to see itself as a longhouse "with the sky as its roof and the earth as its floor."[19] Long before the institutionalization of the confederacy, this desire to live in peace takes the form of the longhouse, "in which there are many fires, one for each family, yet all live as one household under one chief mother."[20] The explanation of how the message of peace was to be disseminated was first delivered to a woman by the name of Jigonsaseh, who had provided the Peacemaker with food and an ear to listen to his message. And because of this, the Peacemaker stated,

> Now it shall come to pass that the woman shall possess the title of chieftain, she shall name the chiefs, that is because thou, my mother, was the first to accept the good news of peace and power. Henceforth thou shall be called Jigonsaseh, new face, and the mother of nations.[22]

According to Iroquoian scholar Barbara Alice Mann, Jigonsaseh was "an emissary, herself, originally from the Attiwendaronks (Neutral Wyandots) to spread the message of the corn, she was the leader of the Cultivators with whom the Peacemaker had to deal if he hoped to prevail."[22] The tradition tells us that these two leaders, the Peacemaker and Jigonsaseh, agreed that peace was the answer and together they strategized and planned for its initiation. This she did under the assurance of the Peacemaker that "the place of women would be ensured in his proposed Great Law."[23]

After their meeting, Jigonsaseh warns the Peacemaker that the direction of his journey will lead him to the fiercest, most damaged, and most dangerous individual known to humanity at that time. The Peacemaker responds that this was exactly for whom he came, to heal broken people in order to correct them in their minds as well as in their bodies.

The Giver of Life, later addressed as the Great Creator, specifies the grounding in the Great Law. The Peacemaker:

> set forth the argument that government is desirable . . . that government is specifically organized to prevent the abuse of human beings by cultivating a spirituality, a spiritually-healthy society, and the establishment of peace . . . and that peace was to be defined not as the simple absence of war or strife, but as the act of striving of humans for the purpose of establishing universal justice.[24]

Paul Wallace tells us that when the Peacemaker left Jigonsaseh, he went in search for the Man That Eats Humans and found him.[25] We are told that when the Man That Eats Humans was preparing to eat, he looked into the kettle and instead of seeing his face, he saw the face of the Peacemaker. Having seen the face of righteousness, strength, and wisdom, he was moved in his heart and no longer had the desire to kill or eat human flesh. This was not enough for the man, however, as he was so plagued by the memory of what he had done. When the Peacemaker finally encountered him in person, he told him:

> Truly, said Deganawidah, what has happened this day makes a wonderful story. Thou hast changed the very pattern of thy life. The New Mind has come to thee, namely Righteousness and Health and Power. And thou art miserable because the New Mind does not live at ease with old memories. Heal thy memories by working to make justice prevail. Bring peace to those places where thou hast done injury to man. Thou shalt work with me in advancing the Good News of Peace and Power.[26]

This journey next brought Jigonsaseh, Ayonwantha (also sometimes referenced as Hiawatha[28]), and the Peacemaker to the land of the chief of the Onondagas named Adodaroh, a great and cruel wizard, who killed and devoured all men who approached him. He was such a terrifying person that the birds flying over his lodge fell dead at his feet, and he was so twisted in his mind, body, and his hair that upon his head lived a mass of tangled snakes.[28] As the Clan Mother emphasized:

> In their approach to visit Adodaroh, Jigonsaseh loaned the Peacemaker her song, which ultimately was able to calm Adodaroh long enough for Ayonwantha to orate the Words of Peace and for Jigonsaseh to comb the snakes out of his hair to straighten his mind.[29]

After his encounter with Adodaroh, the Peacemaker proceeded on his journey to spread the Good News, and the first people to receive him were the Kanien'kehá:kas. They were the first people to take and receive the news of the Great Peace, and accordingly, they are considered the founders of the League.

The narrative concludes with Jigonsaseh placing deer antlers on the heads of the chiefs as a symbol of their authority and giving them the words of the law. The chiefs still wear the headdresses to this day. In contemporary Haudenosaunee tradition, the women, in keeping with the promise of the Peacemaker to Jigonsaseh, explain "the obligation to help achieve peace" and place this headdress upon the heads of the chiefs.[30]

A crucial element in the political life of the Iroquois is the role of the clans in the historical tradition of the Haudenosaunee, which consists of councils working through the problems of relationships to develop the sisterhood of clans.[31] Thus far, we have looked at "stories of origin" dealing with different levels of being: the Creation Story concerns the origin of the cosmos, the narrative of the Three Sisters concerns the origin of life, and the Great Law concerns the origin of social structure. We will now look specifically at the role of the clan mother within Haudenosaunee society.

How a Clan Mother Came to Be

In this section, Clan Mother Iakoiane Wakerahkats:teh shares how it came to pass that she inherited the role of Clan Mother. She begins with the return of her grandmother from Shingwauk Residential School in Sault

Ste. Marie to the Mohawk Reservation at Akwesasne in the late 1800s. Through colonization and Christianity, she contends that there was an erosion of identity among the Haudenosaunee. The Haudenosaunee speak of a chief from the mid-1700s named Sganyadaiyoh (Handsome Lake), who, as a result of colonization, dreamed that the way to retrieve his people from drunkenness was through the "good message" of Christianity. In doing so, he took up a patriarchal attitude and diminished the role of women, even going so far as to order death squads to silence them.[32] The Clan Mother identifies the 1930s as the time when the indigenous community began to retrieve traditional ways:

> It brought us back to a place of ourselves.
>
> My grandmother was part of a movement that went into the communities to identify families that could reconstruct the governmental structure founded on the principles of the Great Law of Peace. They sought to identify women to not only revive the structure, but to retrieve the role of Clan Mothers. As a result of my grandmother having ten kids, the confederacy planted saplings, sometimes in duplication, within the communities to see who would regrow those chieftainship titles. In 1963, my family was condoled into leadership titles.
>
> After my grandmother passed away, my mother, as the eldest daughter, inherited her wampum strands, which symbolized the authority invested in women to stand up [nominate] male leaders. At the time, my mother's eldest brother was still in leadership under the chieftainship title Tehanakari:ne. When he passed away, my mother put my brother-in-law, Ariho:te, in that position and he has sat there for over twenty years. When my mother died, my three older sisters decided that I was the only one eligible to sit in my mother's seat. They handed me her wampum strands and I sat on that authority to nominate for nine years. I was still a young mother with young children and was not really politically minded. I didn't feel like I could fulfill the role as efficiently as my older sisters could. But having married within the same clan, my sisters weren't qualified to sit in that position.
>
> To be qualified, you need to be married to someone of the opposite clan, you need to know our language, and you need to have daughters. I have three daughters and even though my sister had four daughters, she was married to someone in her same clan. They wanted me to be Clan Mother because I

fit the criteria, making it so that fewer people could hack at my roots. I never envisioned myself as a Clan Mother, because I knew how heavy the responsibility is. My sister said if we didn't uphold the title, it would go into the ground with my mother on the day of her funeral. I couldn't let my mother and my grandmother down by letting the title die within my generation after all the work they had done to breathe life back into it. I said I would hold the title until I could find someone else, because in the back of my mind I always thought there was someone else who was better fitting, and so for several years I tried to find another Bear Clan family that could take this responsibility.

Then the Wolf Clan called for a condolence in 2005, and it was at that time that the Wolf Clan chief-in-waiting said to me, "Well, if you're ready, let's move these titles forward." I brought forward my candidates and I was thinking this is the best I can do. Because my brother-in-law had been there for twenty years, I knew he had the experience, history, and knowledge to be there, and I sat my eldest son, Aronhiaies, who was only nineteen years old at the time, behind him so that he could be groomed for the future. You always have to think of those who can fill those spots for the future, so you try to set them in a place of learning and introduction to the duties of a chief. You have to grow them, little by little, as we always knew my son would someday fit the role. I moved my candidates forward and I urged other Bear Clan members to move their candidates forward, but on the day of condolence, nobody put forth alternative candidates. So when we went before the elder brothers, I introduced my candidates. At that point our family could have been vetoed, for whatever reason, but it's not often that chiefs will veto a Clan Mother's decision.

On the day of condolence there was a Bear Clan man that contested one of the Wolf Clan candidates. His objection brought the condolence ceremony to an abrupt halt, and while the younger brothers deliberated, I stepped outside the longhouse and cried a prayer into creation. I humbly asked to not let the ways of the Great Law of Peace end here with us, and, thankfully, the Bear Clan man's objection fell on deaf ears. All of my candidates went through. I thought, at that time, I would do the best I could do but if they didn't

> accept that, it would be alright and I would be free. I wanted to be released of my burden, but to my amazement, they put us all through and they condoled our family into leadership, and here I stand today, as Iakoiane, Bear Clan Mother of the Kanien'kehá:ka (Mohawk Nation).
>
> Frozen in time, I remember the surreal moment when I was no longer one of the people but a Bear Clan matriarch! While I stood in the longhouse with my family, a sudden downpour of rain drowned out the words of the speaker. Steadfast, I stared through a rain-soaked window, enveloped in a moment out of time. My spirit left my fear-filled body, and once again I cast another earnest prayer upward in a spiritual appeal: "Sonkwaiatison (Creator), I don't know why you stood me up here, I am the weakest in all of your creation, I know so little of how it is to be a woman leader among my people. I know even less of how to watch over a chief. But you, Creator of all things on earth, stood me here. If I am to fulfill the duties of Iakoiane and to uphold a life of peace and nobility, then I impart a most desperate request . . . Help me!" Since that moment and prayer, I have been greeted by spiritual beings and guided to the headwaters of ancestral knowledge. A power greater than myself is the guiding force to all the women's work that is now being done in our community.

~

Throughout my discussion with Clan Mother Iakoiane Wakerahkats:teh, I wondered if there was a specific incident that prompted her decision to resurrect the ancient traditions into contemporary practices. Her response was illuminating:

> Apparently, there was some misperception in the community about whether women could attend ceremonies if they were on their moon time.[33] The prevailing understanding was that if women were on their moon time, they were asked to not go to a medicine ceremony. We were told that it was because we are powerful and would somehow inhibit or take away from the potency of the medicine. Women began to start asking about this, about whether they should go to ceremony. What in fact was the belief and position? One

> day, I visited a Wolf Clan faithkeeper to ask for clarification, and he told me what the prevalent belief was, which I questioned further. His response to me was, "Well as long as you women keep coming to ask us men for your answers, we are going to continue to tell you. So, until you begin to take ownership of your own business, we will always be telling women what to do."

This was a turning point for Iakoiane Wakerahkats:teh and she said:

> I realized in that moment I had to roll up my Maxi pad and begin to take ownership for all our feminine issues. He was right. I had to rematriate my worldview: it was the driving force for me to reconstruct the Moonlight Lodge, to gather women under the full moon, to come together in celebration of our bleeding time and our womanhood, to bring all woman issues in the lodge to talk, sing, dance, pray, and feast about, and to begin a process of deep healing for our women.

This anecdote about Iakoiane Wakerahkats:teh awakening to her own predicament, and her decision to "roll up her Maxi pad," appears to be the catalyst that launched her into the powerful work with the women—who are the heart of the nation.

The moon ceremony and moon lodge were resurrected after Iakoiane Wakerahkats:teh had this formative encounter. The moon ceremony and moon lodge are collective celebrations of a woman's moon time, synchronized with the phase of the full moon. Just as ceremony helps the group, so too can it help the individual woman. Clan Mother Iakoiane Wakerahkats:teh contends that if you have a healthy woman, you have a healthy family, and in turn, a healthy community. With this strong foundation, nationhood functions at its highest capacity. In other cultures, and traditionally, the idea of the moon lodge was to coordinate women's moon time and to weave together the immense powers of women's bleeding time. The lodge, in a modern context, has evolved to have a closer relationship to the current realities and conditions of modern-day women. On the whole, it addresses the residual effects of historical traumas experienced through the inherent injuries that women continue to suffer through the generations. Finally, the intention of each moon lodge is left up to the lead conductor, who will interpret the monthly needs of each individual woman and with the group as a whole, in direct relationship to the ever-changing seasons of Iethi'nisten:ha Ohon:tsa.[34]

4

Crossover Ceremonies

The Creator provided us with ceremonies to remind us of our place in the universe, and our responsibilities as human beings.

—Wilma Mankiller, *Every Day Is a Good Day: Reflections by Contemporary Indigenous Women*

Ever since 1492 when the Europeans looked upon our world—they sought to transcribe our languages and our history from a European male-centered worldview. They recorded our history through their written language, only making credible man's experience and perspective. They didn't value or feel the need to record the women's story. I don't know if it's because the men back in the day were trying to protect the women of our nations or if it was the European male mind that didn't consider the women's experience as valid or important. I would suspect that it is the latter. What they didn't realize is they were walking into the place of a matrilineal society.[1]

This chapter is perhaps the most important chapter in the book because it is within these pages that Iakoiane Wakerahkats:teh generously shares with the reader the core and transmission of her understanding of the world. Thus, the chapter first reviews the life stages of Haudenosaunee men and women as they become initiated into full adulthood and participation in the community. Next, it considers the importance of ritual as the community invites, initiates, and sustains the rebuilding of a nation. Finally, the chapter examines in detail two Crossover Ceremonies.

There are seven stages of Crossovers, and while I will be describing each one briefly, the focus for this chapter will be on the fourth Crossover Ceremony that is the transition of adolescence into adulthood. I was privileged enough to witness and participate in the Crossover Ceremony of young men and women of the Haudenosaunee in the months of May and June in 2012 and 2014, respectively.

It is said that it takes a village to raise a child, and customs that celebrate important changes are primary aspects in a child's life. The Crossover Ceremonies I mention earlier are now in their eleventh year of being conducted on the Akwesasne Reservation located in upstate New York.

The work involved to conduct such a ceremony relies heavily on the collective energy of the community and the leadership of Iakoiane Wakerahkats:teh, the community's elders, and a core team of aunts and uncles.

> Within our society we maintain a balance between the responsibilities of the women, the responsibilities of the men, of the chiefs, and of the faithkeepers. All the people in between have to help keep this balance so that at no time and no place does anyone have more power than the rest; for our leadership to function all must have equal power. They must speak to one another.[2]

Although the principal theme throughout these ceremonies is to summon healing energy that focuses on the youth and their growth process toward maturation and adulthood, it is the whole community that experiences healing, for only through the public witnessing and excitement for their cultural life can the ancestral world be reached. This requires a sincere and concerted effort by the village as a whole. To steward cultural competency in the initiate, an aunts' council for the girls and an uncles' council for the boys determines their individual cycle of fasting. As Clan Mother Iakoiane Wakerahkats:teh contends:

> *Enhontonkehte* (fasting) is an honored tradition. The ability to endure deprivation, no food, no water, for the assigned number of days is an essential tool to invoking higher spiritual insight. A young person's intense passion can be tested during a deprived state, making them able to open up to a "meaning of their medicine," that which they need to survive and that which is their gift to give.[3]

Twenty weeks of preparation are divided into four phases: 1) the Calling (calling out youth to participate), 2) Teachings (cultural knowledge), 3) Ritual (subdivided into four phases occurring each year over four years and where each initiate is in the actual ceremony), and 4) Reentry (reentry into the modern world). In Iakoiane Wakerahkats:teh's words:

> We will give them the teachings that every Kanien'kehá:ka man and woman should know. In our sisterhood journey, we will ask for Ehtisoh:ta Asonton'ne:ka Karakwa (Grandmother) Moon to bless us as we reclaim a cultural model for future generations to measure themselves by. Therefore, before we can be well with our daughters, we need to heal our own wounds of maidenhood before we can be present in their ceremony. In healing our wounds, we will make peace with our power. Healing wounds of the heart is best attained in sacred ceremonial space. Our hearts and souls speak in images rather than words, and a moon ceremony creates powerful images to heal our wounds.[4]

The first time that I attended the Crossover Ceremony was in 2012, when fifty-two young men and women were going through the process of initiation. In 2014, I attended again and there were seventy-seven young men and women participating in the ceremony. Both years represented an impressive growth from seven boys in 2005 when the ceremony was originally revitalized. It has become essential, then, that Iakoiane Wakerahkats:teh call upon the community, especially those who have a heartfelt concern for the future of the youth, to help facilitate the process. Members of the community commit to sustaining the young men and women prior to and during their spiritual journey. All skills are welcomed. The young initiates need to hear their Kanien'kehá:ka language, absorb ceremonial teachings, learn ceremonial songs, and know that someone cares. Additional work details (usually for men) include site preparation, woodcutting, shelter making, transport, maintaining fire for five days, and tending to the boys by defusing risk while they ceremony in Brasher National Forest.

Women in the role of aunts nurture the young woman's spirit by counseling and encouraging her during arduous moments. Women mentors are needed to act as role models demonstrating healthy behavior. The young woman learns how to carry herself respectfully as a woman contributing to the nation. Caregivers are needed to support and to mediate communications between parents and children when entering a threshold of ritual isolation.

Life Stages

There are seven life stages within the culture. The first rite of passage is the Rite of Conception, which happens naturally when a man and a woman come together in a place of intimacy, "conceiving and reenacting the creation story."[5] At conception, the mother *Enionttahwa*, or "begins to hold." In the nine months of fetal development, pregnant Haudenosaunee women participate intimately in what the Haudenosaunee consider the second transitional crossover: birth. As midwife Katsi Cook wrote, "Birth is a ceremony, a life-way, that is primary in re-affirming people's relationships to each other, to their environment, all of creation, and to themselves."[6] The Haudenosaunee traditionally say, "He now comes into the inheritance of the land."[7] Iakoiane Wakerahkats:teh calls these stages crossovers, and each of these crossovers has its own rituals and celebrations. Even conception is considered something sacred and is mediated through ritual. Iakoiane Wakerahkats:teh invites her husband into this ritual by stating, "Let's go ceremony." She describes the sacredness of the conception process with humor, but then becomes serious and contends that "when it's done in a sober mind, a straight mind, when it is done with the right intentions, that is the consent of both partners, there is a balance."[8] It is at this coming together, this intimate mindful experience, where conception becomes the medium by which the door opens to guide a spirit in.[9] As Clan Mother Iakoiane Wakerahkats:teh confirmed to me, "We are only spirits passing through a human experience."[10]

Iakoiane Wakerahkats:teh tells me that her grandmother shares the creation story with her as a way of explaining this rite of passage:

> In the garden, after Turtle Man courts Sky Woman's daughter, they lay down in the lodge, feet to feet. It is told that he placed arrows on her stomach, and this was the conception of the twins. In our Creation Story, a father is named, there is no virgin birth. For many in the Sky World, Sky Chief is the father of Sky Woman's daughter who gave birth to the twins. However, in my version, I suspect it's the lacrosse player.[11]

Once the conception occurs and the baby is born, there are still more distinctions to be made. For example, if the baby is born "veiled," it will require more attention.[12] This is because such babies are considered to be healers, seers, and medicine people, often gifted with extrasensory intuitiveness.

Birth for the Haudenosaunee is a natural occurrence involving a huge physical change not just for the mother, but for the one taking his or her first breath of life: the child. The Haudenosaunees' sense and rhythm of nature provides them with profound insights during the time of childbearing.

> For the Haudenosaunee, women, usually grandmothers, are the helpers at birth. They are called Iewirokwas (yeh wee LOH gwas) in the Kanien'kehá:ka (Mohawk) language. This is a cultural title held by Kanien'kehá:ka women who "scoop then from water" or "pull them from the earth" or "pull them from a dark, west place." Essentially, this is what the Moon does. Those of us who are practitioners of birth know what it is to scoop an infant from a puddle of amniotic fluid in order to clear an airway. We know what it is to "call the baby" with instruments of rattle, drum and the power of song and the human voice. We work hand in hand with creation in the moment of birth. Using her ceremonies throughout the cycle of a woman's life, the Moon instructs us with her constancy and her light.[13]

When a child is born, its place in the nation is already established. The children grow into their role—they are given an identity. In this stage, they hear all the concerns of the mother, they speak her tongue, and they learn from her all of the basics of behavior and development. The next stage following birth is the age of wonder and wandering. At this point, the child is curious, enjoys exploring and understanding his or her surroundings and life, and begins the search for self-identity. This particular transition involves great physical changes. For example, a rite of passage referred to as "Toothloss" is seen as the moment when children leave their babyhood behind.

The greatest physical change occurs during the process of puberty and thus needs the most attention as it is the period that leads children into adulthood. Adolescent youth are guided though this transitional phase with great care in the hopes of guiding them to become responsible and caring members within their community.

> In these days, we have many young people who were not born into our traditional way, but after they have the ability to make decisions of their own, when they become mature

> enough to make decisions about what kind of a life they want to lead, they come to our longhouses and have a name given. When they are mature young adults they come with a desire to have a name within our clan and this is given because we rarely turn people away from our longhouse or our way.[14]

Through various rituals, these young men and women are connected to their community that fosters and nurtures the rebuilding of a nation. It is in this crossover ritual that the youth define their place in society according to their gifts through ritual and ceremony. Iakoiane Wakerahkats:teh opens her address to the initiates by stating: "We gather here to remind you that you are our children, you belong to us, we claim you, we are going to do whatever it is that we need to do to build you so that you know that you have some place to belong."

What is intriguing about the crossover ritual for the young is that their spiritual journey during the first four years is supported in the family and the community. They ritualize the individual into a space that allows them to be in acceptance of their transition. Clan Mothers, chiefs, members of the community, and individual families help to guide the rites. The community initiates these young men and women into the place of community, taking the time to explain to them their roles and their responsibility. In this ritual, the first four years are guided by teachings, ceremonies, and the blessings of elders in the context of community witnessing.

Once the first four years of the initiation process are completed, the last three years are completed in what is called "solo time." Now when these young men and women go out to their lodges to pray and to be with Creation, they do so only with the companions of commitment and humility. They are no longer fed, celebrated, or held in the womb of community. It is about having led the young people into a place of creating their own rituals and their own spirituality. There is no festive food, dancing, or words of encouragement. There is no pat on the back. There is no witness to that arduous ordeal that they have to undertake themselves. There is no direction given. It is a self-guided journey of reflection and spirituality.

The next rite of passage, following a child's transition into adulthood, is that of marriage. However, the Bear Clan Mother was quick to mention that marriage is a relatively new concept introduced through Christian imposition. In Kanien'kehá:ka culture, marriage is when "you look for a partner to nest with," which can be a temporary relationship as seen earlier in the Creation Story with Sky Woman's relationships with both the lacrosse player and Sky Chief. Part of this involves the maturity of being able to search for and discern a nesting partner; this is a relationship that goes beyond just the two individuals. Families and clan members also play a role in maintaining the health of these relationships. Iakoiane Wakerahkats:teh's perspective on marriage is as follows:

> Marriage as a rite of passage has suffered a cultural disconnect in the last century, marred with Euro-patriarchal attitudes. The "honor and obey" vow has left a lasting effect on a whole generation of Kanien'kehá:ka women's position and authority. As we became voiceless, the importance of our work in family structure became marginalized and secondary. Marriage was no longer about partnership but about male dominance. In terms of traditional value, the marriage ceremony lost its social importance and ritual significance because our European counterparts viewed it as pagan and not worthy of sanction. It is no longer the standard pathway from adolescence to adulthood for young adults.
>
> When we look at the state of marriage today, it seems to be headed for dustbins as a natural passage in the life course. Marriage is a rare occurrence and is very different than the one our parents or grandparents experienced.
>
> Historically, women set the rules in courtship and marriage. They are the bearers of cultural traditions in marriage. We need only to look to our cosmology and feel the essence of woman as a constant thread throughout our creation story. Beginning with the ordeal of Sky Woman and her journey from the Sky World. The creation story deeply reflects respect for the feminine; Earth as our mother is always in a state of fertility giving forth the abundance of life to nourish us. Women's attitudes and expectations for marriage are an important measure of overall social confidence in the tradition and a weathervane of which way the marital winds will blow.
>
> The traditional belief in the rite of marriage is to enter it with a strong desire and determination for a lifelong and loving partnership. The most important ingredient in marriage is that of respect, not love, as respect in a relationship outlives feelings of lust or love.
>
> Many women are disenchanted with the idea of marriage. Their pessimism reflects a convergent reality. Women need more emotional intimacy, more help with childrearing,

> and a more even division of labor within the household. Women have gained economic independence. As they are better educated and more likely to be employed outside of the home today than in the past, they are not as dependent on a husband's income. Consequently, they are less likely to "put up" with a bad marriage out of sheer economic necessity and are more likely to leave when they experience unhappiness. As breadwinners, wives expect a more equitable division of household work. Thus, the experience of working outside the home contributes simultaneously to greater economic independence and less tolerance for husbands who exempt themselves from involvement with children and the household.

While on the reservation, I heard some men say that they didn't like the elaborateness of the rituals or the fact that they were led by women. When I asked Iakoiane Wakerahkats:teh about this, she acknowledged that although the rituals are facilitated by women who know how to lead the ceremony, she further added that after the four-year crossover rituals, young adults are encouraged for the next three years to enter "solo time" and "solo space" (without the support of the community) to fast and pray. While this "solo time" and "solo space" can be nurtured by the men, they often struggle to self-generate.

> Unfortunately, the men have been unable to self-generate. They cannot organize or guide themselves into that place of humility. They don't know what it is they need to do without the woman. When I think about the work that got started and that continues, there is always criticism. It makes me think about how deeply rooted the ideals of the colonizers remain in the thoughts of our people. The thought that women's leadership is not as good as that of the men. This inequality between men and women is carried through the generations. These are the issues that are on the battlefield. We try to raise our young and show them a sense of balance and cooperation between men and women to help them understand that men and women complement each other. It is not about control. It is about harmony.
>
> In the traditional sense, our ancestors valued the coming together of man and woman as a coming together of two clan families in a state of social prosperity and political

> balance. The families ensured its deeply desired benefits such as sexual faithfulness, emotional support, mutual trust, and lasting commitment. Respect encourages a couple's sexual faithfulness to each other: "Once married, they have no other sexual partner." Divorce is rare in traditional Haudenosaunee marriages.[14]

The next significant physical change is that of menopause. It marks the end of a woman's fertility, the time when a woman no longer cycles with the moon. A transitional ritual is required not only to acknowledge the arrival of this stage but also to recognize her potential new freedoms.

The Clan Mother notes that, at this time, the Haudenosaunee celebrate her and begin to consider her a real leader because she has real-life experience.[15] She can now become a faithkeeper or a Clan Mother because her experience and wisdom position her in such a way that she is able to counsel and address political issues that affect both her individual community and the larger nation. She also has probably acquired economic stability by this time in her life, so she can now begin to give back to her community, a community that has supported her though teachings, medicine, ritual, and leadership in the political forum. This physical change cements the end of fertility, through which she can begin to transfer back wisdom and ancestral knowledge to younger generations.

The seventh and final rite of passage is death. This journey is perhaps the greatest physical transformation. It allows one to *go back to pick berries again* and is, in that sense, not the end of a life but rather an opportunity to be both in Sky World with the Sky Holder and return to Mother Earth until that time when there is an opening to return once again to Earth.[16] The Sky Spirit is what returns to Sky World, while the Earth Spirit returns to rest in Mother Earth, creating the faces that look up at passing women (mentioned by the Peacemaker) hoping to be born again. Any understanding of the afterlife as being solely in the Sky World would be a Christianization of the Haudenosaunee spirituality; thus, fully understanding the two-spirit concept is integral in understanding the Haudenosaunee view of the afterlife. Each life has a breath spirit or sky spirit, and blood spirit or Earth Spirit, and the two must be kept in balance. Joanne Shenandoah, a Haudenosaunee of the Oneida Nation, states, "In our ways, we are taught not to fear aging, death, or what the next life holds. Life is considered a circle. There is so much to be thankful for and to relish in this life."[17]

Healing through Ceremony

> It is hard to see the future with tears in your eyes.
>
> —Kanien'kehá:ka Proverb, in Gerald McMaster, *Native Universe: Voices of Indian America*

The Bear Clan Mother shared the following story with me in an interview on May 18, 2014:

> A childhood friend came to me one day feeling fatigued to the point of exhaustion. Her eyes were sunken with deep dark circles, her body stance was slouched, her breathing was shallow, she sobbed, she trembled, and her voice tone was that of someone who had given up on life.
>
> I could feel that she was looking at death as her only answer. She wallowed in the mud of self-criticism, self-doubt, self-sacrifice, and self-hatred. Doctors could find no physical illness affecting her. She was struggling to survive. Appearing to be separate from her own spirit, there was a time in her life when she consciously gave up a part of herself that she no longer knew how to get back. In our culture, we recognize that there are instances where western methods are not adequate to help treat our people. I was challenged to help her since it seemed as if she had come to me specifically for a reason. She had to participate directly in her own healing process. She needed a process that would fully engage her own healing. A ceremony was needed that would go into the deeper levels of her spirit. Taking in the energy of the moon and tobacco, we journeyed into her pain, visiting her early life traumas. We had to restore her emotional energy and do some house cleaning. And I could see that she was slowly coming back to life.

Interestingly, after the ceremony, Iakoiane Wakerahkats:teh reported to me that there were places within herself where she was also fragmented and needed recovery. And the reality is that she could not help others beyond the place where she had helped herself. And thus, she continues with her ancient practices, bridging them into a contemporary expression, tapping into what she calls her "ancestral connection."

During my ethnographic work on the reservation, I spoke with a number of young men and women who had gone through their Crossover Rituals within the last three years. As a result of their sharing, I conclude that passage retrieval is about reclaiming the essence of who one is by tapping into one's authentic source of power: identity, belonging, and purpose.

> Passage retrieval is a magnificent, heart opening experience that rivals giving birth to oneself. It's about coming home, discovering true fulfillment, showing up and embracing and loving all of our Self.[18]

One young man I interviewed said the following of his experience:

> Imagine what it would be like to not eat food or drink water for four days. My stomach was growling and I felt dizzy; I stumbled when I tried to stand up. Feeling like I was at my weakest point, I wondered if this was worth it. This fast was a tradition ceremony for my culture. It taught me a lot about myself. I learned that I can push myself to the limit and still finish what needs to be done. I learned a lot about life and my part in the world. The greatest lesson I learned was that I am not as invincible as I think I am.
>
> The point of the ceremony and not eating for four days was to purify my body and mind. To shed my childhood. We had to fast in the woods by ourselves; it was a very tough challenge mentally and physically. Being alone with no one to talk to and nothing to do drove me crazy the first two days. Then I realized all the things that I have taken for granted. Family, friends, food, water, and these things I had missed. Being solitary in the same place also played a big role in building mental strength. Although I went on this fast alone, I felt like I had built a bond with the other men that had fasted at the same time as me.[19]

One young woman who participated in the Crossover Ritual in 2006 had the following insight to offer concerning her experience:

> Don't give up on it. It seems really hard, but you learn so much and it takes away all the hardness. It's not all about

the food while you are out there. It's more about the other struggles you had to get through and how to get through them.

I learned that I can be alone and that there is nothing wrong about being alone. I learned to have pride in myself, to feel good about myself, and that I can accomplish a lot.

I am Wolf Clan.[20]

She was further reminded of Iakoiane Wakerahkats:teh's words:

Do not speak to your own story, just mirror it back. Ask yourself, "Why am I so afraid to be alone?" Walk with fear. Talk to fear. Do not let it live inside you. Be in relationship with it. Do not let it go. Do not get overinvolved with other peoples' stories. We need to find acceptance, forgiveness, new beginnings, new relationships. We have to be in balance . . . watch the sunrise. Ask yourself: "What is being asked of me? What am I prepared to give?"[21]

Finally, Iakoiane Wakerahkats:teh counsels the young men and women to give love to all others.

In addition to facilitating the Crossover Ritual for young men and women, Clan Mother Iakoiane Wakerahkats:teh is also called upon to facilitate the naming ceremonies. I asked Iakoiane Wakerahkats:teh to explain this:

A mother, either while pregnant or after the baby is born, will come to me in search of a kasenna'on:we, which is what we call an ancient name, for her child. This name will then be placed within the clan structure, the frame of our Nation. Once you're bestowed with a name, our people will begin to identify to whom you belong and what roles and responsibilities you have within that larger structure. One's name may carry a generational family name, or if the family name has been forgotten or severed in some way, the family will come to me. They will bring me tobacco. And after the baby is born, I will retrieve the elements of nature within the birth story that pulls the baby from the waters. Then that spirit that has asked to be born will be guided here on its journey, whether it is wind, fire, animal, journey, or a person, that element will be identified on that baby's birth. It kind of becomes that baby's roadmap. So, when I'm naming the baby, I'll put the tobacco under my pillow and I'll sleep on that tobacco and dream of that name, then inside a harvest or midwinter ceremony, I'll name the baby and the clan families will witness this name.

We don't know why this baby was born to this clan, but from this day forward we will call this baby by this name, and we attach this name to the medicine and to the elements, to keep this baby strong so it can fulfill his or her mission in life. We compile the names on a written document that records at which ceremony, under which clan, and under which Clan Mother the naming took place. I also have to know and remember those names that I've given out, for once a name is given out under the chieftainship title, that baby will align itself to my family specifically. And if my chief falls, there is a whole lineage there that can take on the duty of leadership. We call it the basket of names, so if someone in my line passes on, they can't take that name with them to the Sky World, so I'd retrieve that name and put it back in my basket of names, so when a new member of the family comes along, I could return the name back to the family. So, there's a lot of work and planning and memorization in the names that are given.

It's like that one mother who came to me to name her son and when I asked about his birth story, she told me in the evening and afternoon when she would go outside and walk around her fields. She knew she was having a boy, and every time she would go on her walk there would be a series of animals that would come to the woods' edge to gaze upon her walking: the deer, the rabbit, the fox, the birds, the squirrel. All of these animals would stand at the woods' edge and watch her walk. That story alone tells me that the boy will either be a hunter or someone who protects those animals by working in something like conservation, to be someone who saves them from extinction. So, I gave him the name Rowahkehtotah:ni, which means "they look upon him." He comes from a long line of hunters and he has that name, birth story, and purpose. If I were to identify that animals were dying, I'd remember that birth story and call upon that young man to see what he thinks should be done.

I've given over one hundred names since 2005, but not just in my clan. There have to be roughly ten thousand names floating around in our confederacy. It is my responsibility to know our chiefs' names, the characters in our story, the other

> Clan Mothers . . . our population is large, and I also have to know those names in other languages. When a Clan Mother confers someone's name within the clan, that very action confirms his or her citizenship among the Haudenosaunee.

The Clan Mother also emphasized:

> We claim exemption from both U.S. and Canadian citizenship. We don't identify with either. Our community predates any of those nations. Before they drew an imaginary line through our territory. So, we claim Haudenosaunee citizenship because our territory was here long before.[22]

I asked her if this was recognized as legal. Her response was as follows:

> Yes, it becomes legal, but it is not recognized by the United States or Canada. It is up to the child's parents to give their children a saltwater name. My parents' generation all gave us saltwater names so that we had the choice of either using our Okwehon:we or saltwater name. Long ago, our people signed a two-row agreement with the Europeans. We refer to this as the ship and canoe, and the agreement was that we would create a relationship where we would share the resources and the river of life equally, we will govern ourselves in accordance with our laws and our ways, we will not interfere in each other's governance. And so, you can use your Kanien'kehá:ka name, and that is your canoe name. That is the name you use in ceremony or among your own people. But when you are out in the saltwater world, and you know how dominant the ship of the saltwater people is, you use the saltwater name.[23]

The Crossover Ritual for Young Women

> Weaving a new cover on an old story.
>
> —Iakoiane Wakerahkats:teh

The Clan Mother shares her reflection, written in her words, of her own sacred journey:

Perched on the end of a solid oak couch my uncle Mahises (Moses), a Bear Clan chief and medicine man, would reminisce about the old days and interpose stories about Iotsitsison, a beautiful celestial woman that fell from a hole in the sky. She was the carrier of all life. Her constant presence was a soft wind that blew upon my long brown hair and a calling that often stood me in a steadfast gaze at the heavens, looking for that opening in the sky and wondering if she would fall again someday.

All the years growing up in the longhouse I never heard not ever a whisper about this glorious woman. Why was she taboo and why was I, as a woman, taboo to the culture I grew up in. In the midst of my grandma years I find myself on an earnest journey to find these answers and to find the woman that fell from a hole in the sky.

With a bundle of determination, I began to go in search of Iotsitsison. Someway, somehow, I had to weave a new cover on an old story. The only way I could do this was to enter into the spiritual consciousness of woman and create sacred space inside a sweat lodge. A mysterious place I have seldom entered without skilled conductors. I questioned my own ability and even talked myself away from this journey several years before a visit with a Mayan holy man at Tom Cook's 2010 Sun Dance finally sent me on my right course. "The ancestors say you are lazy yet your flame burns bright and the ancestors gather quickly to be at your fire"; in a serious voice "they say you wait too long to be in ceremony, you make too many excuses and you should be in a ceremony at least once every twenty days."

The powerful message followed me home and it still took several months of excuses before I finally committed to a moon vigil that would sequence for thirteen full moons. I feared ceremonial commitment because it seemed to be too much work, but my greater fear was to disobey the ancestors.

For Haudenosaunee women, the cycle of the moon determines their yearly calendar. The changes with each passing moon indicate times for hunting, planting, gathering, and ceremony. And women naturally carry thirteen moons within their being (in accordance with the moon cycle).

As a woman I had to bring myself to that point where I would give myself permission to embark on this journey.

It seemed strange that the final push I needed was a man's permission giving me the authority to do my own work. I had to change this way of thinking.

I felt great uncertainty and somehow knew I could not venture into the unknown alone so I called upon konon:kwe (all women) to accompany me. Daughters, sisters, aunties, grandmas, friends, and any other woman who could find her way to the door of the lodge was welcomed in. A quiet place to remove her mind from the overpackaged clutter of product marketing and messaging; a safe haven without shame, judgment, or expectation burdening her gentle spirit; a holy place to grow her own nourishment and to harvest her own bounty within creation.

Each month we women gathered to be one with each other during the transformative power of the full moon. Detaching ourselves from duties of family as we retreated to the moon lodge to be in the company of sisters, a time to honor and weave ourselves in Sisterhood. I started to orient myself in this sacred space and I started to call it the moon lodge.

The only door of the lodge faced east and an altar connected the entrance to a sacred fire lit by caring firekeepers. In a circle around the fire we would gaze into the luminous face of Sky Woman's daughter as she rose on the night horizon during each full moon. Adorned in long skirts and shawls, we gave thanks to creation, elevating our calling in our sacred tobacco and singing our moon songs as we bathed in her potent light. Each woman joining me in sanctified bearing and without question as to why I went in search of a celestial truth held by a celestial feminine.

Our firekeepers took great care with our grandmothers (the rocks) as they awaken their energy in the intense flames of the sacred fire that lit the entrance to our moon lodge. Our grandmothers were greeted in as "the ancient ones," the ones who hold in their illumination woman's knowledge. Deep inside the belly of the lodge a sphere of immense darkness and a pungent smell of Mother Earth sent us back in mother's womb.

With humble breath, in a language given to me by my mother, I ask for pity from the ancient ones as their images dance in the fervor of a radiant glow. Surrounded by my sisters, we sat in the shadow of their immense energy as I called forth all women descended from their wombs. With great calling we sing, and our voices ascend beyond the roof of the lodge. Soon we are swept up in a vortex of massive night sky just floating toward the magnificent light of the Iotsitsison (the moon), and her black shawl sparkled with stars. Captured in the medicine of time, we release all the burdens our bodies collected during the lunar month and we renew our energy by reconnecting to Mother Earth's powerful fertility.

The culture of our ancestors gave great power to the moon. My Ista's (mother's) wisdom told me that babies are born by women and by the moon. The unborn faces of the generations yet to be are called forward by the moon, and the moon's magnetic pull makes the oceans bulge and rivers flow. She calls into being all plant life and she controls our fertility. Ista's wisdom had to be made real for my daughters and granddaughters. She told me how important it is to place yourself in sacred space during bleeding time. Women are the carriers of abundance and fertility, and bleeding time meant you down fended [removed] yourself from the rest of community. It was a time to dream, to find spirituality and reflect upon your life.

By the third moon I began to honor this own sacred journey by acknowledging my intuitive knowing inherent from the experience of my mother, grandmother, and great grandmothers. Finding trust in the feelings emerging from my lunar cycle became my medicine as it guided me to see into the future of my unfolding journey.

The moon lodge soon became a social web of phenomenal women respecting and honoring themselves and each other by returning every full moon to reconnect themselves to a powerful source. In the beginning, we had to come to terms with our own blood and bleeding time. I had to reassure a woman that it was okay to be on your cycle inside the moon lodge. It made the lodge even more powerful, for the dreams and visions of bleeding women can bring vital messages such as planting, healing knowledge, and guidance on community relations.

Our story of Sky Woman tells us that it was she who brought life and set into motion our ceremonial cycle. Our sacred seeds were carried here under her fingernails, and now we carry the spirit of those seeds in our wombs. We need to trust in our Sky Woman. When questions need to be answered, we sit in the lodge and ask. People can benefit through the powerful gifts received during a women's moon ceremony from inside the lodge.

Visions and dreams emerged, a kind of intuitive knowing found only in women during their times in the moon lodge. Sky Woman and our ancient grandmothers helped us to recall the old ceremonies long forgotten, such as the Crossover Ceremony for our sons and daughters.

Culture today separates every sector of society from honoring cycles of earth and sky; long ago forgotten . . . until now! As granddaughters of Sky Woman, we dream during our bleeding cycles, her powerful presence joins us every full moon, honoring us with her healing light to fill our spirits. We know that there is a woman's wisdom within our wombs that needs to be found, celebrated, and espoused, to a rightful place in our busy lives.

The spirit of Sky Woman calls to us from a distant heaven to teach us ways of honoring and healing the earth. It is no coincidence that she feeds our dreams at this time, when the earth is in dire need of healing. We must return to ceremonies of honoring if we want to heal our earth and ourselves. Answers crucial to our survival can come through women and the moon lodge. Our bleeding time is a time of incredible power, we must give ourselves permission to ask for the wisdom that eludes us. We need to set into motion our own ability as women and create the social change that needs to happen for our daughters. The grandmothers know all the answers and they will help us remember everything we need to know, just as they helped the generations of women before us. Our moon lodge is a safe haven for women to come together in sacred space to honor and celebrate our cycles under the fullness of a full moon.

The moon lodge helped me metamorphose with my sisters, to share our gifts and pass women's wisdom on to our daughters. The moon lodge allowed us to live within the cycles of the earth and moon. By honoring and celebrating our wombs, we found Sky Woman. By remembering her, Iotsitsison, we remember ourselves. She helped us recreate our women's ceremonies in a time to bring loving relationships to all woman and children on earth. We became sisters in spirit in the moon lodge. Perhaps, eventually, moon lodges will once again become respected women's places in communities.

The healing journey continues as I hand over the power of the lodge to women who participated during my thirteen-moon vigil. In the coming lunar year every sister initiated in the lodge will now take her turn to do the calling of our sacred Sky Woman. My vigil to recall Iotsitsison gave me many struggles in which I found incredible strength. Perhaps my greatest struggle was in giving myself permission to make my bleeding time a time of ceremony and to shed the taboos that have made me feel less than a man. I can feel for the first time that I am not taboo in the life-giving flow of my own blood. I now sit in common with my sisters as I see a new conductor bloom in the power of the moon lodge. Waksot:sen. "Yes, grandma moon is in me," and I am glorious with my blood and my fertility.[24]

The Crossover Ritual for young women begins with a few remarks from Iakoiane Wakerahkats:teh that state the intent of the gathering:

As we begin to swim in a sea of female consciousness, we state our intention clearly, and in the coming days we will project our reality to become what we have announced it to be. Our intention for our daughters is to bestow moon time teachings upon them that will call them to new levels of responsibility and accountability as they grow into womanhood. The wisdom of our grandmothers knew that coming into womanhood had to be a guided journey. We are co-creating a monumental event, and as we experienced the pain of its birth, we will push it forth to be a lived reality. In its conception we will reach back to heal past wounds while looking ahead to bring forth a new vision. In the timeless space of ceremony, everything becomes possible as we rescue the fragmented pieces of our culture.[25]

These opening remarks are then followed by the "words before all else" (a litany of gratitude for all of Creation), and a tobacco burning helps those present to focus on the intent of the day. The purpose is to call upon the moon and the ancestors to be present in this womanhood ritual that will transform their daughters from young girls into mature Kanien'kehá:ka women. The young women gather with their mothers and aunties and are gifted with a beaded moonstone necklace with the face of the moon, carved out of the base of a deer's antler. The antler is a symbol of the chief's authority, a position that has been bestowed upon him by women. The girls are asked to pick a stone from a basket that contains one word on it, and they are asked to reflect on that word. It may be truth, family, humility, health, among others. Then the girls are asked to spend time journaling. Past initiates speak to the girls about their own experience. The girls are also given a moon basket, with tools that they might need such as flint and tobacco to pray with, and are instructed once again on the symbol of authority, the deer antler. They were advised to wear their moon necklace as a reminder of their spiritual connection to Grandmother Moon, their source of strength and power for their journey. As Iakoiane Wakerahkats:teh states: "You give a man voice. It is you who give a man leadership. Men walk aimlessly until a woman gives him direction. Do not be afraid of your power, the power that you are to gain these days."[26]

From there, they begin to awaken the seed within the girls. The girls stand with their mother and grandmother, while each of them take turns in giving them words of encouragement. They are reminded not only of their uterine line, but of the power that lies within their womb. Iakoiane Wakerahkats:teh kneels before each girl and prays for the children that are to come. She emphasizes that the awakening of the seeds ceremony is not meant to have the young women go and have unreflective sex, but instead to have a consciousness and a chance of selectivity in "who you choose to let in that door. Do not let there be trails of footprints in your field of snow. Ensure that whoever enters this sacred door asks permission before entering."[27]

In order for the girls to not feel so isolated or alone, they are invited to call in their grandmothers, and to see the grandmother of their people in the face of the womb. In evoking the mother's line, older women in the opening ceremony recite:

> We have come into this world through a woman's body and our cells and souls carry the memory of her within, even if we never knew her. We are connected to all women who ever walked this earth. Like them, we cycle every month. We share this intimate experience with them. In cycling, we are one. As cycling women, we are no longer confined by roles defined by men. We are all souls in a woman's body, aligned with the moon and tides, bleeding and catching our blood

> monthly or conceiving children. Through the power of our extraordinary blood we are all made equal; we stand in the image of the first woman, Iottsi'tsi:son.[28]

They stand in a circle with a red yarn that is passed from girl to girl with the purpose of retrieving their uterine line. And so they begin with their name and then name as many women in their personal matrilineal line that they can. Iakoiane Wakerahkats:teh reminds them that the remembrance of this uterine line is symbolized by the red yarn wrapped around their wrist and is to be worn throughout their fasting.

> The red yarn symbolizes in this ceremony the web that binds us together, it is the uterine line, the sisterhood of women, connected. Our strength lies in holding each other close. We are all women, we all bleed, and it is this that gives us voice. Someday, your daughter will stand here, with this same fire, and call your name. And this immortalizes you.[29]

And with this, the daughter begins her chant of the Moon Song.

Daughters of Sky Woman Song

I:I ne Tsiotenhari:io Okwa:ri ni waki'ta ro:ten
I am beautiful Cornsilk, and I am of the Bear Clan
Kanien'keha:ka wa kat ton wi son
I am a Flint woman
Iethi'nisten:ha ohon:tia katonhwareha':tie
My canoe drifts on Mother Earth
Atonhnhetshe':ra kawis
I carry the breath of Life
Konkwe'ti:io tan:non ke'shats te
I am beautiful, I am strong
I:i waka terien ta:re
I have inner knowing
Iah tektsha:nis tsi tewahkaweh ha:tie, ne akoweh:ia
I am not afraid as I paddle my canoe along
Watiatanonha:kies tsi naho:ten wakaterienta:re
I am all that I know
akenekwen:sa wehn ni ta ra tsie Watnawi:ne
My blood flows and drifts with each moon

Io hon tia re'shens tha ne ohon:tia
It fertilizes and energizes the earth
Ka'onwiio ne ka'onwii:ne
The beautiful canoe that floats along

Mothers Response Chant

I:se Tsiotenhari:io Okwa:ri ni sen'taro:ten
You are beautiful Cornsilk of the Bear Clan
I:se ne Kanien'keha:ka sah ton wi:son
You are of the Flint people
Iethi'nisten:ha ohon:tsia sathonwareha:tie
Your canoe drifts along Mother Earth
I:se ne Atonhnhetshe':ra sawis
You carry the Breath of Life
I:se ne sonkwe'ti:io tan:non se'shatste
You are beautiful, you are strong
I:se saterienta:re
You have inner knowing
I:se ne iah tesateron:ni tsi te sathonwareha'tie
You are not afraid as you paddle along
Ne sa ia'tanonha:ties tsi naho:ten saterien ta:re
You are all that you know
Watnawi':ne tsi naho:ten saterienta'
All that you know flows
Sanekwenhsa wehn ni ta ra tsie Watnawi:ne
Your blood flows and drifts with each moon
Ka'onwiio ne ka'onwii:ne
The beautiful canoe that floats along

At this point the grandmother invites the girls to what is called "the uncles' walk," which is where the uncles check the lodge one last time and offer words of encouragement to the young girl. When the lodge has been secured, then the girls are brought to the white teepee to change for their sweat, which consists of their aunties, their mothers, and other women from the community. The moon lodge can be comprised of one to three rounds of prayer and teachings. In the sweat, the mother tells her daughter her birth story. At the end of the sweat, the aunties are asked to leave the moon lodge. As Iakoiane Wakerahkats:teh states: "The moon lodge is a mirror reflection of our Creation Story and where we do our purification." The mothers remain and offer their daughters words of encouragement, and the rebirthing is reenacted with the mother pushing the daughter out of the moon lodge into the aunties' arms, who rock her in a beautiful Pendleton blanket. As the mothers exit themselves, they go to their daughters and once more speak words of encouragement and affection. The girls are veiled, for now they have entered the fast. They are brought down to the lake to be cleansed and washed and then change into white clothing before going into their fast. The covering or veiling ensures that they will not reconnect with the mundane world until they have finished their fast. There is no talking or contact once they enter the sweat. These young men and women space the fasting and prayer in order to receive the insight and messages from the ancestors. At the threshold entry, aunties sing their nieces to their lodges, in a lunar formation, moving counterclockwise as they release each girl one at a time to enter the threshold of her sacred space.

The most essential ingredient of the girls' rite is the sacredness of the girls. Residing between two worlds, in sacred space, they too are sacred. They embody the divine and have in them the power to heal. This part of the ceremony puts much attention on their bodies. Before and after seclusion in a fast they will bathe them. After the fast, they step over a threshold into their new state, and the celebration begins with bathing, body painting, massaging. There is much emphasis placed on washing and combing, maybe cutting their hair, arranging it in a more mature style. The bathing is a joyful social gathering of female relatives who splash and dunk the girls in water while Ista or Tota prepare dry clothes for them to fast in. Before and after the fast along with the cleansing, ritual bathing, and purifying, there will also be a moon lodge ceremony. At the end, the girls will towel dry and wear clean women's clothes. The girls are helped to realize a new body image, that of a woman, not a child. The girls are then dressed and painted as they return to the main camp. The change inside them is made visible for all to see and witness.

At the threshold retrieval the aunties sing nieces out of their lodges. The aunties will once again circle the earth lodge counterclockwise to gather the nieces and return them to the earth lodge. A reentry ceremony will take place, which will include the moon lodge, a bath, hair combing, and a new dress.

The next stage is what is known as dream guessing:

> After purification, she returns to earth and tells the elder women about her dreams, visions, or spirit within her lodge. Through dreams experienced during such a period, the dreamer

> could be granted *orenda*, magical power, and a guardian spirit or power animal.[30]
>
> The final ceremony is about giving gratitude.
>
> The ceremony will end with an all-night social led by the young men and women at the longhouse, with invited relatives and guests. Uncles and young men will sing for the young women. A big ceremonial cake is baked in a hole in the earth and served by the young girls to everybody after the heart is given as an offering to say nia:wen to Ista Ohontsia and Tota (Grandmother) Moon. Finally, the girls have "walked into Beauty" as young women.[31]

Wearing Clan shawls with domes, flowers, or moons on them, the girl becomes the center of attention of her clanship and her community. Younger girls watch her being celebrated, stepping over the threshold, and look forward to their turn.

> And the mothers and aunties danced with her. We shall all dance for a month, until Tota Moon gets full again. It is a big time when a girl comes of age; a happy time.[32]
>
> One young woman wrote the following about her experience:
>
> In a way, the rites allowed me to find myself without realizing it. Every year was hard but to me, because I was so intuitive and I dreamt a lot, and I wasn't here spiritually and mentally, I had to struggle with encounters, and being alone was a huge thing for me, especially alone at night in the dark. Just my mind playing tricks on me: seeing things, I just didn't know how to handle it, you know? I just didn't know what to do. I came to face a lot of fears in my life and a lot of things that I didn't want to deal with, in myself. I cried a lot out there because there was just so much that I carried. Even though I was young, I carried a lot. So, that was probably the low point . . . experiencing those messages and those lessons, accepting it and learning from it too. Learning to not be so angry, releasing those angers and creating a positive thinking. That was probably my second or third year, because I never did the twenty-week prep time. I was so stubborn and last

> minute, and at that time I felt like I didn't want to do it, but as soon as I did it, I knew I needed to do it.
>
> It was just something inside—a kind of realization. Probably one of the highlights of my fourth year was that I realized that, after three years, I should be more prepared. I changed a lot—I was here on time. That was a good year, even though it rained a lot, even though I froze, all of my stuff was wet, and I couldn't light a fire. You know, emotionally, psychologically, it was a good year for me. Learning to accept my life here, to accept my family. You know, I needed the women. Even the way I carried myself, I felt like such a changed person. You just feel so different from when you walk in, or the year before.
>
> There is no right or wrong answer going through this. Although it is a test, you're going to get answers for you, not for anybody else. You're not just a number; you're not just a name. People care about you and are here to help the initiates find out who they are as a youth and as an individual. I actually have a niece participating this year, and I think that the best advice I can give is that you get what you put into it. If you're here all of the time, then you're going to get a lot out of this, and you're going to experience a lot, and you're going to have so much to be appreciative for. Always use your medicines and pray with gratitude that you're here today.[33]

The Crossover Ritual for Young Men

After months of preparation, the Crossover Ritual begins at sunrise, where an eagle's call gathers the people. Iakoiane Wakerahkats:teh begins the Crossover Ritual for young men by reminding them that these are ancient tests of strength and endurance. The ritual begins with the rising star, and the burning of tobacco as a way of recognizing and sending intentions to the ancestors. She addresses herself to the mothers, affirming that what they want for their sons is to be strong, to be their own person, to treat women with respect.

Iakoiane Wakerahkats:teh says:

> It's hard to let go, to release your son. But you will know that you did a good job when he steps into his manhood and never looks back. The reason we have strong men is because

> we have strong women who raise them. And it is easier to raise a strong boy than to repair a broken man.[34]

And then she turns to the young men and says: "The only true weapon we have is to love you. That's all we've got."

Tentatively listening to Iakoiane Wakerahkats:teh, the boys sit with their baskets before them containing the blankets, firewood, and flint that they will need during their time of fasting. The mothers and sons sit across from each other, the main fire between them. One by one, each boy is asked to approach his mother and sing "his song." The mother places a headband around his forehead emblazoned with the insignia of his clan and is given the opportunity to present him with words of encouragement. After the bestowing of this clan symbol and the sharing of support and commitment, the community drives to Brasher National Park to release the boys for their fasting. The mother carries the young boy's basket for the last time. The women of the community accompany the boy to the park and down to the river, and in this sacred place Iakoiane Wakerahkats:teh reminds the young men of the waters of life. She tells him that they are like the pine tree, strong, tall, holding up the sky. She reminds them, "Like this tall tree, the winds will blow strong, but you will not fall."

This is followed by all of the women dipping branches into the lake and blessing the boys. From the lake, the women accompany their sons up the hill, where all of the men and uncles are standing strong in waiting. Each mother steps up before the uncles with her son and makes a request of the uncles to teach her son to be a man. And with this, the women in the background sing the traditional release song.

The mother's release song basically speaks of the mother's readiness or willingness to let her son go. She lets her son go so that the uncles might teach them their ways, reminding her son that she will always love him. And when the last mother makes her statement and the women of the community sing their release song, the boy is given to the uncles. They are encouraged to go with the uncles, singing their power songs, and to not look back to their mother, looking for her pity. I watched the men as they went into the woods, their song ringing through the trees.

Inside the uncles' circle, the ceremonial activities begin with a sweat, prayers, and songs to deepen the letting go. After the purification, the uncles guide their nephews into a sacred world where the landscape and the plants and the animals become their teachers. Each year, the young men are exposed to different environments in nature, and the uncles help them recognize plants, rocks, landmarks, and paths.

I am told that this is the process that initiates the fasting, whether it is from one to four days and nights with no food or water. While the boys are in their individual lodges across the woods, the uncles remain in a central location in case of an emergency. The young men will have no direct contact with anyone but his uncles, which only occurs in the case of an emergency.

The Clan Mother clarifies that "he is encouraged to create simple, self-generated ceremonies, to make the night an all-night vigil, staying awake in a self-constructed circle of stones, cedar, or cattail, that is at once a tomb and a womb."[35]

> The same way that the young man went into his fasting, he returns to his community after purification in the sweat lodge. This is meant to give the young man the opportunity to integrate what he has discovered, his newfound medicine, into his life. His uncles can either explore the meaning of his experience, or let him be without analyzing it, taken on a case by case basis in accordance with the young man's need. A significant council to the young men by the uncles is that while it takes an immense amount of courage to embark on this journey, it takes even more to return.[36]

A young man reflected:

> When I returned home, everyone greeted me and told me how proud I had made them and what a good thing I was doing. A meeting was held where everyone gathered to see the boys who set out four days ago. We all gathered around a ceremonial fire and listened to the stories of all our experiences and feelings. I spoke of how I felt about not eating. The aching, weak feeling of hunger. The shock I got when I was too thirsty to think of anything but water. Thirst was my biggest challenge; it controlled my every thought and made me feel like a fish out of water. Loneliness sets in immediately after being dropped off in the woods. It is only magnified when night sets in. Then you realize, you are not alone, there is a world of life around you. I couldn't see it, but the sounds kept me up late at night. I set an example for younger boys to follow and to live a good life. I showed younger boys that were starting their fast that you can push

> through anything, and that if I could do it they could, too. It was a humbling experience when a younger boy asked me what it was like to fast and how he was excited to do what I had completed. That day I felt like everyone was looking up to me and they were proud to say that they knew me. I was welcomed back from the woods, in the eyes of my people, I wasn't a kid anymore. I was welcomed back as a man.[37]

Family members are also keen to recognize the metamorphosis that their children go through after participating in the rites. One mother shared the following:

> My son is in his third year, and I've seen a lot more maturity and responsibility from him. Some of the challenges in the Crossover Rituals were on my part: releasing him, letting him go. The first year, I cried for hours. It wasn't a bad thing. I was letting go of my little boy and when he came back, he was going to be my young man. The way he stood and handled himself with confidence showed me how big of a difference there was. My son's father was addicted to drugs and hasn't been a part of his life since he was four years old. My son asked my brother to be one of his uncles, and seeing the closeness that has developed between them has meant a lot to me and is something that I am very proud of. It has also brought me closer to my brother. Their responsibility shows in the words that he speaks, how he holds himself, and how he is more respectful and caring.[38]

One young man who completed all four years of his Crossover Ceremony said:

> I am age eighteen (as of 2010). I just finished four years of preparation for my rite of passage. I wish to share my experience and journey of four years, how my mother and my uncles helped me through and how they taught me the ins and outs of my language and culture. More importantly they showed me who I am and what my true identity is.
>
> In my first year, I was scared. We started off in the mountain where it was rainy and cold. I was only thirteen and didn't really know what I was getting into at the time. There was one point I was lost, not knowing who I was. There were

seven of us. We were released from our mothers and released to our uncles to guide us in coming into manhood. I learned how to survive as a young man in this world without electricity or heat. The uncles took over and had to guide us down a path where we hit many hurdles, blocks, and dead ends. They would help us get over the difficult path. If we wanted to quit, they were right there. They would tell us what to do or what to expect. It was almost like another chapter in my life. I began to realize where I came from, where my family came from, as a Kanien'kehá:ka, not only as a Kanien'kehá:ka, but as a Haudenosaunee. We are a special people because we were here on Turtle Island first. We participate in the rite of passage to bring our people back and show them who our true identity is. The young today struggle with assimilation. They say we are Kanien'kehá:ka, but that's not all that we are. We are Haudenosaunee.

In this process we choose our uncles; your heroes, who you see, respect and want to be like. That's how I chose my uncle. You are allowed to have as many as you want. The more, the better. You can't just follow and put all the weight on one guy's shoulders; it's better to have all the guys, you have more variety. Some guys may know this and another may have a better way to explain something else, it's stronger that way. As I went along, I tried to have less guys, but it was more on me, to learn more by myself. It was more independent. Year after year, I tried to go with less uncles so that I could do it myself, to show my mom, my aunts, and my uncles that I could do it myself instead of have them guide me all the time. I don't think anyone really realized it. They thought I was just slacking and not getting uncles there, but I wanted it like that.

The first challenge was trying to stay dry. That first weekend all it did was rain. We thought it would never stop raining. It was so cold out. That was our main struggle, to stay dry.

The first year we had a lot of stuff. My backpack was stuffed with a couple pans, a lot of food, firewood, matches, a tarp, a sleeping bag, and a blanket. I was pretty prepared that first year. I felt like I was just going camping. At the beginning, we were pretty close to each other physically; I could see the other guys. As the years go one, you get more

> and more spread out. The first year you stay with the uncles. One night and one day. And you just add one day to that every year. By the fourth year, it is four nights and four days.
>
> The uncles are all at one sacred fire on the outside. They keep that fire going for us and they always keep tobacco in there. And they make sure we are alright.
>
> As I said before, I was a little scared. I was nervous. I had never stayed outside in the woods by myself before that. It was like opening a new year with new things to come. I put that tobacco down to have new things come toward me or to give me a message. It was something different, I had never done that before. I learned from that.
>
> Every morning, just before the sun comes up you work your way to the river where the main fire is with the uncles, and they have to watch you because they have to listen. It's not that they don't trust you, but they need to make sure you are doing everything right. If you get injured, they can come get you. But when you are out there and you come back, you can't say anything, you can't talk when you come back. It's like you are isolated, you can't say one word to your uncles. It's hard but you learn from it.
>
> The first year was on the mountain, the second year was at the swamp. Where I was, it was really wet, that's why I picked it. I wanted to see something different from the woody area. Compared to the woods this has more bugs and mosquitoes. You find different medicines.[39]

One theme that emerged many times in the interviews was not only the transformation in the young men and women but also the healing that took place within families and generations. The changes in these young men were confirmed by many mothers and grandmothers. What follows next is a reflection from one of the grandmothers:

> I am a grandmother to a seventeen-year-old. He has been in my life since he was about three. His father was killed when he was young; it was a great struggle for my daughter to stay strong after losing her child's father. This is his third-year release and it is still very emotional. I noticed that when he came back a year ago I did not have to remind him of things, he just did it on his own. He was more responsible, and it took a big weight off of me. I started doing less and he started

> doing more. I saw growth and change. He heard about this through his friends. They were telling each other that the rites were an awesome opportunity to prove themselves, to get out and to survive. Like the reference to the corn husk, when you are peeling back that husk every year, you are exposing more of a young man. That is the symbolism of what we did this morning when we bathed him, clothed him, and then passed him to his uncles.
>
> My boy has never had an issue with his identity. He has always identified himself as Haudenosaunee, and it has always been the foremost identity in his life. He is proud that he can speak our language and he carries his culture with him.
>
> I think that this has been a great opportunity for my grandson to incorporate all of the cultural and linguistic elements. I too am learning from this. He just wants to learn all he can about his culture, and the rites allow him this opportunity.[40]

The grandmothers and mothers reiterate the importance of initiating their boys into adult roles within the community. In the words of Edward S. Curtis:

> Embracing the role of keepers of culture, contemporary Native American women are taking responsibility for maintaining the heart of their traditional cultures against the TV age. Many are attempting to maintain circles of their Native communities in the midst of urban sprawl, provide their children with tribal identity to help them resist assimilating pressures of public school, and even bridge the chasm for North American Indian who had no Native upbringing. The tasks may have changed, but the work of being a Native American woman is as challenging as ever. Native American women will persevere, as they have for thousands of years, in an imperfect world, shaping life out of what is there.[41]

Iakoiane Wakerahkats:teh names her hopes and desires for the young men and women in a similar way:

> I think my hope is to have them capable of calling out their medicine, to realize what their true gift is, and to realize why the creator sent them here. My hope is that they will find

their medicine and bring it into its fullness by sharing it. The end result of this experience is that they become productive citizens of our Nation. There is also the hope that when we get old, they will tend to us as they will tend to the coming generations.[42]

5

Indigenous Strategies in the Global Arena

It is hard to see the future with tears in your eyes.

—Mohawk proverb, in Wilma Mankiller, *Every Day Is a Good Day: Reflections by Contemporary Indigenous Women*

This book has offered a tiny slice of the life of the Haudenosaunee people and has focused on Iakoiane Wakerahkats:teh's desire to retrieve significant ancestral wisdom to help rebuild her nation. It would be remiss to not say a word about the context that surrounds her efforts. As Tonya Gonnella Frichner, a lawyer and activist of the Onondaga Nation, writes:

> The need to support the cultural survival of Indigenous peoples and to defend their human rights is the consequence of centuries of colonization, colonialism and dominance, including dispossession of their lands, territories and resources and subjection to unjust laws and policies.[1]

According to the 2013 U.S. Census, approximately 5.2 million people identify as Native American or Alaskan Native, with 80 percent of those identifying as such living off of reservations.[2] There are currently 566 federally recognized tribes within the United States.[3] Many indigenous activists argue that the consequences of globalization are the modern counterpart to the effects of the conquest in the mid-sixteenth century.[4] As a result of the excesses and abuses of globalization, indigenous populations have been greatly impacted worldwide. A ray of hope is the emerging indigenous movements found throughout the Americas that struggle to preserve their culture and their heritage. Within these pages, I have provided a representative case study contextualized within the native experience of decolonization and the response of the Haudenosaunee to reclaim their ancestral traditions.

Many indigenous people outside of the Haudenosaunee have formed their own organizations and are actively seeking to improve their sociopolitical and economic reality. As a part of its contribution to the World Decade for Cultural Development, UNESCO has encouraged the cultural expression and activities of indigenous people. While I am aware that there is a great deal of difference between what has been written and what has happened at the practical level, it is important to document the fact that the United Nations has received indigenous leaders and is being made aware of the fact that human rights address not only individual rights but collective rights such as humanity's obligations to the Earth. This particular theme of caring for the Earth is one that indigenous people have carried with them in their cultural memory and are now intentionally articulating publicly through various public addresses, which is what the Clan Mother herself is also attempting to do through the medium of this book.

Historically, the 1970s were the decade for the emergence of marginalized communities (e.g., African American, Latino/Chicano, women's movements, the American Indian movement) and was also the time during which many of them found their voices and began to advocate for their human rights. By entering into the international arena, the world was made aware of the disturbing reality that indigenous people were: living shorter lifespans; suffering because of substandard health care, education, and high unemployment; and facing the environmental destruction of their lands and waters as a result of mining and other extractive industries.

The Indigenous peoples' representatives have engaged the international community lifting up their critical life issues since the early 1980s. With the birth of the Working Group on Indigenous Populations (1982), the indigenous movement became recognized within the United Nations system. In conjunction with the significant bodies of the United Nations working from 1994 to 2006, the United Nations General Assembly adopted the UN Declaration on the Rights of Indigenous Peoples September 2007,[5]

> a positive move toward creating true reform to fully respect the right of Indigenous peoples to sovereignty and self-determination, and the right to free, prior and informed consent when it comes to state, corporations and/or extractive industries designed to exploit their lands, territories and resources.[6]

On December 10, 1992, designated as Human Rights Day, the official opening ceremonies for the International Year of the World's Indigenous Peoples was held at the United Nations in New York City. At that gathering, twenty leaders from indigenous nations from all over the world came to address the General Assembly. This was significant because it was the first time in history that indigenous peoples were able to bring their issues directly to an international body.

Oren Lyons, faithkeeper of the Onondaga Nation of the Haudenosaunee, in his address to the assembly provides an insight into his nation by referencing the Great Law of Peace:

> We were instructed to create societies based upon the principles of peace, equity, justice, and the power of the "good mind." Our societies are based upon great democratic principles of authority in the people and of equal responsibilities for the men and women. . . . Our leaders were instructed to be men with vision and to make every decision on behalf of the seventh generation to come.[7]

After providing the assembly with a sense of his people, Lyons continues:

> We were told that there would come a time when the world would be covered with smoke, and that it would take our elders and our children . . .
>
> We were told there would come a time when we could not find clean water to wash ourselves, to cook our food, to make our medicines, or to drink, and there would be disease and great suffering . . .
>
> We were told that there would come a time when tending our gardens we would pull up our plants and the vines would be empty. Our precious seed would begin to disappear. There are some specific issues that I must bring forward on behalf of our nations and peoples . . .[8]

With this eloquent opening, Oren Lyons spells out the various issues that affect his people, which include, but are not limited to: the violation of treaties, the refusal to recognize and support religious freedom, the appropriation of intellectual property, violence against women, and, of course, the basic rights of water and land. Ingrid Washinawatok-El Issa, a member of the Menominee Indian Tribe of Wisconsin, writes: "Virtually every Indian community has a struggle of some kind or another, yet some of the most pressing issues involve defending the earth."[9] She cites the struggle of the Navajo against the removal from their lands, in Nevada a struggle between the Western Shoshone and the Bureau of Land Management, the Lummi of the Northwest Coast are trying to stop the clear-cutting of forests, and "in the East the Mohawks of Akwesasne are fighting the smelters and other heavy industries that have virtually destroyed the St. Lawrence Seaway and surrounding regions with toxic wastes and heavy metals, poisoning the reservation's water supply and lands."[10]

Despite placing these very difficult issues before the General Assembly, Lyons presents the global community with alternatives and options, prompting us to remember that we need "to have the courage to change our values for the regeneration of our families and the life that surrounds us."[11]

He concludes by referring to the Two Row Wampum Treaty, stating:

> Even though you and I are in different boats—you in your boat and we in our canoe—we share the same river of life. What befalls me, befalls you. And downstream, downstream in this river of life, our children will pay for our selfishness, for our greed, and for our lack of vision.[12]

Today, humanity still struggles with greed and a lack of vision. At a meeting held at the United Nations on September 21, 2014, indigenous people gathered once again to address climate change and the survival of Mother Earth. Native peoples issued their plea to protect the Earth, warning that "there is no more time for discussion on preventing 'Climate Change.' That opportunity has passed."[13] They argue that we have passed the point of discussion because the air, water, plants, animals, and all others upon the Earth are not the same anymore. They issue their passionate plea underscoring that "all that is Sacred in Life is vanishing because of our actions. The truth is [that] we have moved beyond climate change to survival on Sacred Mother Earth."[14] In order to rectify the situation, the Council of Elders believes that we must restore the sacredness in ourselves and honor our obligation to care for all life in our discussions, decisions, and actions, and by instilling respect into our very culture.

This commitment to values of interdependence and respect is witnessed in contemporary movements that focus on some of the more serious challenges facing indigenous communities, such as undemocratic legislative strategies, water rights, and resource extraction. Canada and the United States are two countries that pose grievous challenges to their native populations. In Canada, undemocratic legislative strategies include the Safe

Drinking Water for First Nations Act that raises serious constitutional and discrimination concerns as it forces native communities to give up human rights in order to enjoy safe drinking water.[15] Resource extraction is another challenge facing native communities in Canada, which is clearly evidenced in the cases brought to court by the Kitchenuhmaykoosib Inninuwug and Wahgoshig First Nations "regarding the inappropriate involvement of resource companies on their territories."[16] One result of the tireless struggle of indigenous groups is the case of the Canadian Supreme Court's ruling against Chevron regarding their deliberate dumping of eighteen billion gallons of toxic waste water and seventeen million gallons of crude oil into the Ecuadorian Amazon. The ruling is a major victory for both human rights and corporate liability as Chevron is now legally obligated to carry out a full-scale environmental cleanup and provide potable water and health care to the communities it damaged.

In the United States, the issues faced by native communities range from sovereignty and recognition to child welfare issues. However, access to drinking water is also a challenge even with the Bureau of Indian Affairs. Recent litigation undertaken by the Hopi tribe against the Bureau of Indian Affairs has resulted in increased efforts by the Environmental Protection Agency (EPA) to protect drinking water supplies in the area of the Tuba City open dump, which was used in the 1950s and 1960s to deposit radioactive materials. Due to the litigation, the EPA will now closely monitor the wells on the site and the conditions of the drinking water being sent to the Hopi village of Moenkopi.[17] With President Barack Obama's reelection in 2012, federal policies toward indigenous people have remained stable, including the addition of the American Indian Health Care Improvement Act. Yet the United Nations Special Rapporteur on the rights of indigenous peoples also notes that while policy trends toward indigenous communities over the last few decades should be lauded, we still need to implement a strong program of reconciliation that will "resolve to take action to address the pending, deep-seated concerns of indigenous peoples."[18]

This interconnection between nature and indigenous culture globally and more specifically within the Haudenosaunee is manifested in their traditional knowledge. It is their traditional knowledge that is the basis for both their spiritual growth and their intimate commitment and relationship with the land. I began this book by stating that there were three major contributions that the Haudenosaunee people have made to those of us who inhabit Turtle Island, particularly those of us living in the United States. First, we are indebted to the Haudenosaunee for providing the framework for our own democratic processes and government.

The Iroquois Confederacy has the distinction of having the world's oldest continuously functioning democratic government in which women wield equitable power.

Second, the American people were inspired by the Haudenosaunee's demonstrated acknowledgment and respect for women and their place in society. At the 1990 Continental Meeting of Indigenous Peoples held in Quito, Ecuador, the approved resolutions of the Women's Commission again articulated that "the invasion of non-Indian values has drastically changed the relationship between men and women and the role that women play in the communities and nations."[19]

Finally, we look to the Haudenosaunee as a source of wisdom with which to reshape our understanding of and relationship with the Earth. Kanien'kehá:ka (a well-known midwife by the name of Katsi Cook) reminds us of this relationship and interdependence when she beautifully states:

> Women are indeed the first environment. We are an embodiment of our Mother Earth. From the bodies of women flows the relationship of the generations both to society and the natural world. With our bodies we nourish, sustain, and create connected relationships and interdependence. In this way the earth is our mother, the old people said. In this way, we as women are earth.[20]

The understanding that indigenous women's lives are intertwined with the natural world was echoed at the World Women's Congress for a Healthy Planet (1991), specifically, the International Indigenous Women's Caucus. At that caucus, international indigenous women reaffirmed the significance of their own creation stories that had emerged out of their individual cultural traditions and homelands, which continue to nurture and give them meaning today. Their message is accompanied by the responsibility to care for the Earth as their mother. The Women's Caucus contended:

> As indigenous peoples, we are witnessing the destruction of our sacred Mother Earth. The suffering and pain of Mother Earth is felt by us as if it were our own. She is being destroyed, as we are being destroyed, at a rate in which it is impossible for healing and renewal . . .[21]

The women argue that to cease this environmental destruction, humanity must embrace a morality predicated upon the laws of the natural world and recognize that the honoring and protecting of the diversity of life must include not only the plant and animal world but also the diversity of peoples. In this sense, diversity must also include spirituality, cultures, and all ways of life.

Indigenous peoples are sensitive to the human role of harmony and balance in the world. The 1991 International Organization of Indigenous Women echoed once again the wisdom of our ancestors in relation to our relationship with Mother Earth:

> As women of the indigenous peoples, our lives are intertwined with the natural world. Our myths of creation tell the story of our emergence from the earth, which continues to give us nurturance and the reason for our lives. We are inseparable from the earth out of which we were created. As indigenous peoples, we have lived on this land for tens of thousands of years in harmony and equilibrium with all of nature.
>
> We depend on her for our sustenance; we depend on each other mutually for the development of our lives, and we are interrelated both physically and spiritually. As human beings we have a responsibility to take care of each other and to take care of nature.[22]

This statement, articulated from an indigenous and feminine perspective, makes clear that humanity is intertwined with the breathing pulse of all living things. Their assertion further demonstrates gratitude and an understanding of the inseparability of the land with whom we exist. The statement acknowledges our dependence, in a positive sense, toward the Giver of Life, for whom one lives.

Our Oldest Home

Earth is our first, oldest home. Yet many contemporary societies experience a homeless feeling often articulated as not belonging. At times this homeless feeling is concrete. Many people in third world and developing countries have literally lost their homes. Many indigenous people, the poor, and women have been displaced from their homes.

Larry Rasmussen, a renowned environmental ethicist, argues that this homeless mind is a condition of modernity itself: "*Oikos*, as the experience of belonging somewhere intimate to one's bones, eludes most moderns."[23] It is a psychological condition that accompanies development and modernization.

Even apart from homelessness as a matter of mind, it is quite literally a displacement. The highly mobile rich, living from hotel to suburban lot to condo and hotel again, hardly have an enduring community they consider their own, even less a binding commitment to a neighborhood. Many industries recruit workers by selling them the idea that the world is their "oyster." Every locale is at their disposal, but no particular location is home in a deep, settled sense.

I now pose the question: would reclaiming the knowledge that the earth is in fact our first and oldest home have an impact on the experience of displacement and alienation that many contemporary people feel? This ancestral memory is embedded deep within us. If we are to recall the wisdom of that memory, we must stand firmly on the earth and in reverential silence recall the interdependence and intricate relationship we have, not just with the world, the earth, the land, but with the universe. As Teilhard de Chardin, renowned paleontologist, reminds us, humans are the universe reflecting upon itself. As such, consciousness and awareness of the Earth as our shared home provide a sound starting point for this reflection.

Awareness of our common birth home initiates our understanding that the Earth, this sacred place on which we stand and on which we make our habitat, holds for us the secret of our relationships. In other words, our relationship with the earth is the context of all contexts. Many of us do not begin with this global insight, but with our particular, culturally conditioned experience of home. The indigenous traditions teach us that when we separate our existence from the processes of the landscape, our hearts become fragmented and all that is "other" is objectified.

Noeli Pocaterra Uliana is of the Wayuu people from Venezuela and is a member of various Native American organizations such as the National Indian Council of Venezuela and the International Commission of Women of the World Council of Indigenous Peoples. She contends:

> In our vision of the world, it is not possible to speak of a family without restoring the role of our elders as the spiritual guide, as the standard for our conduct. We must restore the role of a woman, as a fighter, as a wife, as the reproducer of life, and the key to preserving the identity of our peoples. The young . . . are the continuity of our people, and it is they who are our own life. It is not possible in the name of Western science and technology that we should ignore the place of the family and the family of communities of the planet. We cannot ignore Mother Earth and the cosmos, who are the sources of life and have been throughout the history of all peoples.[24]

Our indigenous brothers and sisters remind us that the land is the source of our nourishment, survival, identity, and indeed life. Therefore, the contemporary ecological crisis must impress upon our consciousness a new awareness of our dependence upon the earth and each other. We must help our communities understand that we share a common destiny that is linked with the earth because we belong to the earth. It calls for the reembracing of values laden with the heartfelt meaning of our interconnectedness with creation.

This interdependence could provide a resource for new ethics. Returning to the insights of the indigenous women quoted earlier in this chapter, we learn:

> We believe that it is our responsibility to take care of the earth, as if she was our mother. As daughters of the indigenous people we witness the destruction of the land. Our sacred mother is being violated by the devastation of the forests and the mineral evacuations; she is being poisoned through toxic wastes and radioactive chemicals, and we her daughters and sons are being destroyed. We feel the pain and suffering of our Mother Earth as if it were our own.
>
> The most difficult challenge will be to move away from the sole interest in individual lifestyles and ethnocentrism to a more adequate structural and systemic concern; a concern for humanity and the Earth.[25]

As Clan Mother Iakoiane Wakerahkats:teh and the aunties and uncles of Akwesasne work to rebuild their nation by investing in their youth, they are sustained by the memory of their ancestors. This remembrance of who they are and who they are connected to makes the line between past, present, and future not as distinct as it is for those in Euro-American culture.

> Native women know the sacred places generations of their people have gone for renewal and for ceremony. They know where great battles were once fought and where their people held meetings to discuss momentous decisions about war and peace. They have a special relationship with the land where their ancestors sang their songs, told their stories, and were returned to the Earth for burial. This is their homeland.[26]

This is our motherland.

Conclusion

In this book I chose to focus not on the effects of oppression, but on the processes of true cultural healing and resilience, as mediated through the first-person voice of Iakoiane Wakerahkats:teh. Through her voice, readers are invited to witness the uniquely effective role of ritual as a means of gaining access to precolonial worldviews, and of adapting them to contemporary practices.

Native Americans remain unconquered, having resisted Western domination and penetration, fought the loss of ancestral lands, and demanded a voice in their own affairs. Native Americans persevere despite living in some of the most brutal regimes in the world, surviving under the most economic strain, and resisting national and international pressure to exploit every natural resource at their disposal.[1]

Daily indignities suffered at the hands of the dominant group call attention to a litany of injustices in a system of domination, exploitation, and oppression. A journey toward healing must engage critically in "epistemological hybridism." According to Eduardo Duran, the literal translation entails

> being able to think or see the truth in more than one way. Epistemological hybridism takes the actual life-world of the person or group as the core truth that needs to be seen as valid just because it is. There should never be a need to validate this core epistemology or way of knowing by Western empiricism or any other validating tool. To do so is merely a form of neocolonization that will only add to the problem.[2]

This way of perceiving the world creates a new borderland space filled with a new meaning of self-in-community, which bridges and balances two or more opposing worldviews. Again, this is another way of speaking about the mestizaje previously mentioned in the introduction.

No one living in society is free from all forms of ritual. Ritual and ceremony are elements and expressions inherent to being human. Ritual is not an activity without purpose but rather is the way in which human beings construct their worlds. It is also a means to gain epistemological access.

Jennings argues that there is a poetic function of ritual. He contends that first, ritual action is a medium to attain knowledge. It may function as a mode of inquiry and discovery. What this means is that the participants discover who they are in the world and how the world can be reconstituted. This ritual knowledge is gained through bodily action, which alters the world and the place of the ritual participant in the world. It is primarily corporal rather than cerebral, primarily active rather than contemplative, primarily transformative rather than speculative.[3] There is an incarnate character of ritual knowledge that is gained through embodiment.

Life is founded on the door through which we all enter, the mother's womb. Anyone who has existed or will ever exist has come through that door. There is an underlying, implicit similarity between Iakoiane Wakerahkats:teh relationship (as a woman) to the Wolf Clan faithkeeper (as a man) and the struggle between indigenous worldviews and the rational materialism that was so prejudicial to them. Whether it is a question of gender relations, or the clash of worldviews, we learn the same lesson: as long as we turn to a hostile epistemology for validation of our experience, we will always get the same disempowering answer. Thus, empowerment begins with accepting responsibility and validating our own personal experiences as Iakoiane Wakerahkats:teh has articulated for herself as both a Native American and as a woman. This dialogue between them is not only amazing but illustrates the depth of the Wolf Clan faithkeeper's integrity, as well as the integrity of Iakoiane Wakerahkats:teh.

Appendix 1

Letter to Jeanette Rodriguez from Wakerahkats:teh, Bear Clan Matron

Wakerahkats:teh—Iakoiane
Akwesasne, ON K6H 5R7

September 16, 2010

Jeanette Rodriguez
Professor
Seattle University
Department of Theology and Religious Studies, Women and Gender Studies
901 12th Ave, P.O. Box 222000
Seattle WA 98122

She:kon/Greetings:

The old ones spoke of a time when women of the earth would gather during the time of corn harvest. In prayer mothers would unite their voices, lifting it in song to pierce the sky and ask for pity on behalf of their children for the great change that was upon them. The Life Blood of Our Nations–Women's Gathering held at Akwesasne in Mohawk Nation territory August 27th, 2010, is now the historical wind to usher in the weathervane of change.

In a rare invitation, Jeanette, we brought you into the heart of our nations. In a circle you sat in prayer with traditional medicine women as they addressed the place of indigenous women in a modern world.

Time is urgent as we stand in this pivotal point in history. The message has been spoken and it must flow to all corners of the earth.

The old ones chose you, they brought you to us. We cannot bring insult to their request. Without haste the matrons of our nations appoint you to assemble the words for all to hear. There is no monetary reward offered for the work. In return, all there is, is honor. For you will stand esteemed in a circle of chosen indigenous mothers who are guiding in the great change. A Mothers covenant will flow up through the plant roots of earth. Your gift to master words will bring to life a supreme law to undo the injustice of women and children. Your participation is not only important but necessary to the lifeblood of our nations.

In Spirit of Mothers,

Wakerahkats:teh
Bear Clan Matron

Appendix 2

Tasks and Responsibilities of a Clan Mother

1. Must have a clan.
2. Whomever the clan member (family) feels earns or lives the role.
3. Must be of the Mohawk Clan.
4. Must be or have been married to an immediate nation.
5. Must be a "mother" or have children.
6. Must always remain "neutral" on any issue of importance.
7. Must always set a good example for her clan.
8. Must never "vote" in foreign elections or meddle in their politics.
9. Must constantly advise her chiefs concerning the desires of her clan.
10. Gently, the Clan Mother takes the chief outside to talk to or reprimand him.
11. The Clan Mother gives two warnings. On the third warning, the chief is dehorned she will assign men to release him.
12. Must never fail to raise a (new Clan Mother, new chief) within ten days after the death of one of them. If a condolence cannot be carried out at the time, the Clan Mother must at least present the clan women's selection to the Chiefs Council within the specified ten-day period.
13. Must always handle the wampum of her deceased chief and only passes the proper Indian name to her new chief. In case of death,

she sends a runner with a purple ribbon to the younger brother to let him know of the death.

14. Must meet often with her clan, in her own home if necessary, to discuss all matters that concern her clan.

15. Must attend all meetings of importance, namely, Chiefs Council, Grand Council, Clan Meetings, and People's Meetings.

16. Must study, learn, and teach the traditions, customs, language, the Great Law (Gayanerekowa), and ceremonies of her nation to all who listen.

17. Must teach and pass on to her successors all the matronly duties involved and be available.

18. Must always keep the interest of her clan/nation at heart.

19. Must know the Iroquois Confederacy names of her sachem and sub-chiefs and be able to recognize their proper wampum Heads of Authority.

20. Must live as close to the teachings of Deganawidah (the Peacemaker) as possible.

21. Must demand her chiefs keep her informed of all meetings; must communicate on what was discussed at meetings.

22. Must assist and officiate in all name givings in her clan.

Seskehko:wa 25, 1999. September.

Notes

Introduction: The Call of the Earth Mother

1. This is the name by which indigenous people refer to themselves. It means "People of the Flint."

2. "Iakoiane" is a Mohawk title that translates to "she has noble ways."

3. To be considered "condoled," a Clan Mother must go through a high ceremony that is witnessed by other indigenous leaders. According to the Haudenosaunee Confederacy, there are forty-nine Clan Mothers within their traditional system. The Haudenosaunee Confederacy, "Clan Mothers," accessed September 11, 2015, http://www.haudenosauneeconfederacy.com/clanmothers.html.

4. Clans are comprised of families that are bound together by a shared female ancestry. Members of one clan are considered family members, and as such intermarriage in the same clan is forbidden. The clans are named after animals that give special assistance to the people. Clanship identity is of central importance to the Haudenosaunee. Syracuse Peace Council, "Who Are the Haudenosaunee?," accessed June 15, 2014, http://www.peacecouncil.net/NOON/culture1.html.

5. Kanien'kehá:ka Council of Akwesasne, "What Is the Kanien'kehá:ka Council of Akwesasne?," accessed January 15, 2014, http://www.akwesasne.ca/about.

6. See "The Constitution of the Iroquois Nations: The Great Binding Law, Gayanashagowa," Portland State University, accessed June 13, 2014, http://www.iroquoisdemocracy.pdx.edu/html/greatlaw.html.

7. Jeannette Gurung, "Gender Dimensions of Biodiversity Management: Cases from Bhutan and Nepal," *Biodiversity in the Hindu Kush-Himalayas International Center for Integrated Mountain Development* 31 (1998): 98–107.

8. The term "mestiza" as defined by Gloria Anzaldúa in *Borderlands*, as quoted in Jeanette Rodriguez's *Our Lady of Guadalupe: Faith and Empowerment among Mexican-American Women* (Austin: University of Texas Press, 1994), 62: "Indigenous like corn, the mestiza is a product of crossbreeding, designed for preservation under a variety of conditions. Like an ear of corn—a female seed-bearing organ—the mestiza is tenacious, tightly wrapped in the husks of her

culture. Like kernels she clings to the cob; with thick stalks and strong brace roots, she holds tight to the earth—she will survive the crossroads."

9. Wilma Mankiller, *Every Day Is a Good Day: Reflections by Contemporary Indigenous Women* (Golden: Fulcrum, 2004), xxviii.

10. Elsie Paul, Paige Rabmon, and Harmony Johnson, *Written as I Remember It: Teachings from the Life of a Sliammon Elder* (Vancouver: University of British Columbia Press, 2015), 5.

11. Ibid.

12. Edward S. Curtis, *The North American Indian: The Complete Portfolios* (Cologne: Taschen Books, 1997), 22–23.

13. The International Indigenous Women's Caucus at the World Women's Congress for a Healthy Planet, 1991, https://www.nativeweb.org/papers/statements/women/healthyplanet.php.

14. Mankiller, *Every Day Is a Good Day*, 14.

15. Dustin Mulvaney, ed., *Green Politics: An A-to-Z Guide* (Los Angeles: Sage, 2011), 225.

16. Paige Rabmon, "Introduction" to Paul, Rabmon, and Johnson, *Written as I Remember It*, 10.

17. Ibid., 3.

18. Ibid.

19. "The VI Latin America Encounter of Pastoral and Solidarity Work with Indigenous Peoples," *Journal of Promotio Iustitiae* 2 (2006): 33–34.

20. Paul, Rabmon, and Johnson, *Written as I Remember It*, 13.

21. Michael V. Angrosino, *Doing Cultural Anthropology*, 2nd ed. (Long Grove: Waveland Press, 2007), 5.

22. Ibid., 12.

23. George Rawson, "We Limit Not the Truth of God," in *The New Century Hymnal* (Cleveland: Pilgrim Press, 1995), 316.

24. Renee Jacobs, "Iroquois Great Law of Peace and the United States Constitution: How the Founding Fathers Ignored Bear Clan Mothers," *American Indian Law Review* 12.2 (1991): 498.

25. "Tribal Names and Meanings," Native History Memory, January 25, 2013, accessed May 8, 2014, http://www.nativehistorymagazine.com/2013/01/tribal-names-and-their-meanings.html.

26. Robert Venables, *The Clearing and the Woods: The Haudenosaunee (Iroquois) Landscape—Gendered and Balanced* (Philadelphia: Springer Press, 2010), 25.

27. Leila R. Brammer, *Excluded from Suffrage History: Matilda Joslyn Gage, Nineteenth-Century American Feminist* (Connecticut/London: Greenwood Press, 2000), xiv.

28. Sally Roesch Wagner, "Haudenosaunee Women: An Inspiration to Early Feminists," in *Sisters in Spirit* (Summertown: Native Voices, 2001), 50.

29. Eric Noyes, executive director of the American Indian Institute, personal communication.

30. Bear Clan Mother, email message to author, February 4, 2010.

31. Taiaiake Alfred, *Peace, Power, and Righteousness: An Indigenous Manifesto* (New York: Oxford University Press, 2009), 8–9.

32. "Iethi'nisten:ha Ohon:tsa" is a Mohawk phrase that translates to "Our strength, our Earth Mother."

33. What the Clan Mother is referring to by using the term "rematriation" is women's role in the political processes of the Nation as codified in the Great Law.

Chapter 1. Setting the Context

1. Carlos Guzman Bockler, "Memoria Colectiva: Identidad Histórica y Conciencia Étnica en Guatemala," *Revista Mexicana de Ciencias Políticas y Sociales* 27.103 (1981): 194.

2. Wakerahkats:teh, Clan Mother, interview by author, tape recording, Akwesasne, NY, May 27, 2012.

3. Jeanette Rodriguez and Ted Fortier, *Cultural Memory: Resistance, Faith and Identity* (Austin: University of Texas Press, 2007), 108–111.

4. The word "Iroquois" comes from a French version of a derogatory Huron Indian name meaning "Black Snakes." Syracuse Peace Council, "Who Are the Haudenosaunee?," accessed June 15, 2014, http://www.peacecouncil.net/NOON/culture1.html.

5. José Barreiro, ed., *Indian Roots of American Democracy* (Ithaca: Cornell University Press, 1992), 36.

6. Eduardo Duran, "Liberation Psychology as a Path towards Healing Cultural Soul Wounds," *The Journal of Counseling and Development* 86.3 (2011): 10.

7. Wakerahkats:teh, Clan Mother, interview by author, email message, June 3, 2012.

8. Leanne R. Simpson, "Anticolonial Strategies for the Recovery and Maintenance of Indigenous Knowledge," *American Indian Quarterly* 28.3–4 (Summer and Fall 2014): 373.

9. Wakerahkats:teh, Clan Mother, interview by author, email message, May 13, 2013.

10. It is important to note that healing does not, in this context, refer to the healing of the self. Throughout this book, healing refers to cultural, social, and environmental healing, which impacts a larger community.

11. A. James Wohlpart and Peter Blaze Corcoran, eds., *A Voice for Earth: American Writers Respond to Earth Charter* (Athens: University of Georgia Press, 2008), 54.

12. Anna J. Willow, "Images of American Indians in Environmental Education: Anthropological Reflections on the Politics and History of Cultural Representation," *American Educational Research Journal* 34.1 (2010): 67–88.

13. Please see the work of Brenden Rensink, "Genocide of Native Americans: Historical Facts and Historiographic Debates," *Dissertations, Theses, & Student Research, Department of History* (2011), paper 34, http://digitalcommons.unl.edu/historydiss/34.

14. Wakerahkats:teh, Clan Mother, interview by author, tape recording, Akwesasne, NY, May 27, 2012.

15. Herbert Hirsch, *Genocide and the Politics of Memory* (Chapel Hill: University of North Carolina Press, 1995), 16–17.

16. Chief Jake Swamp. "Remembering the Ancient Path: The Original Instructions and the Earth Charter," in *A Voice for Earth: American Writers Respond to the Earth Charter*, ed. A. James Wohlpart and Peter Blaze Corcoran (Athens: University of Georgia Press, 2008), 1.

17. Barreiro, *Indian Roots of American Democracy*, 37.

18. Bear Clan Mother, email message to author, May 13, 2013.

Chapter 2. The Epoch of Sky Woman

1. John Bodley, *Cultural Anthropology: Tribes, States and the Global System* (Mountain View: Mayfield, 2000), 30.

2. Barbara A. Mann, *Iroquoian Women: The Gantowisas* (New York: Peter Lang, 2006), 31.

3. National Museum of the American Indian Education Office, "Haudenosaunee Guide for Educators" (Washington, DC: Smithsonian Institution), 6–7.

4. Mann, *Iroquoian Women*, 30.

5. Ibid., 33.

6. Ibid., 30–31.

7. Ibid., 31.

8. Ibid.

9. Chief Jake Swamp, "Remembering the Ancient Path," 54–61.

10. Venables, *The Clearing and the Woods*, 24.

11. Ibid.

12. Ibid., 25.

13. John Mohawk, *Iroquois Creation Story: John Arthur Gibson and J.N.B. Hewitt's Myth of the Earth Grasper* (N.p.: Mohawk Publications, 2005.)

14. Tom Porter, *And Grandma Said . . . Iroquois Teachings as Passed Down through the Oral Tradition* (Indiana: Xlibris, 2008).

15. Personal interview, May 28, 2012.

16. "Native Peoples of the Region: Oral Tradition," Great Lakes Information Network, accessed February 14, 2014, http://www.great-lakes.net/teach/history/native/native_6.html.

17. Mann, *Iroquoian Women*, 60.

18. Joan E. Rockwell, "The Meaning of Old Age from Native American Haudenosaunee (Iroquois) Women's Perspective: Then and Now," unpublished master's thesis, M.A.I.S., Marylhurst University, 2006, 49.

19. Mann, *Iroquoian Women*, 223.
20. Ibid., 220.
21. Ibid.
22. Ibid.

Chapter 3. Clans and the Epoch of the League

1. The symbol for peace that the Peacemaker left for the Haudenosaunee was the Tree of Peace, and above the tree Deganawidah (the Peacemaker) placed an eagle, which symbolized watchfulness.
2. Renee Jacobs, "Iroquois Great Law of Peace and the United States Constitution: How the Founding Fathers Ignored Bear Clan Mothers," *American Indian Law Review* 16.2 (1991): 497.
3. Ibid., 81.
4. Jacobs, "Iroquois Great Law of Peace and the United States Constitution," 500.
5. Mann, *Iroquoian Women*, 116–117.
6. Wakerahkats:teh, "A Position Statement from Iakoiane Wakerahkats:teh on Behalf of Rotisakrehwa:ke" (N.p.: 2011), 2.
7. Information gathered from the curator at the Iroquois Museum, Howes Cave, NY. Please also see www.Iroquoismuseum.org/ve7.htm.
8. Tom Porter, *Clanology: Clan System of the Iroquois* (New York: Native North American Travelling College, 1993), 3.
9. Ibid., 5.
10. Ibid.
11. Ibid.
12. Akwesasne Notes, ed., *The Basic Call to Consciousness* (Rooseveltown, NY: Native Voices, 1978), 34.
13. Mann, *Iroquoian Women*, 36.
14. Jacobs, "Iroquois Great Law of Peace and the United States Constitution," 498.
15. Akwesasne Notes, ed., *The Basic Call to Consciousness*, 31.
16. Paul Wallace, *The Iroquois Book of Life: White Roots of Peace* (Santa Fe: Clear Light, 1986), 39.
17. Ibid., 40.
18. Akwesasne Notes, ed., *The Basic Call to Consciousness*, 33.
19. Ibid., 35.
20. Wallace. *The Iroquois Book of Life*, 40.
21. Ibid., 41.
22. Mann, *Iroquoian Women*, 36–37.
23. Ibid., 37.
24. Akwesasne Notes, ed., *The Basic Call to Consciousness*, 33.
25. For a more traditional version, please see John Arthur Gibson's *Concerning the League: The Iroquois League Tradition as Dictated in Onondaga* (Syracuse: Syracuse University Press, 1992).

26. Wallace, *The Iroquois Book of Life*, 43–44.

27. Bruce Elliott Johansen and Barbara Alice Mann, *Encyclopedia of the Haudenosaunee (Iroquois Confederacy)* (Westport, CT: Greenwood, 2000), 161.

28. Ibid., 45.

29. Wakerahkats:teh, Clan Mother, interview by author, email message, May 13, 2013. In other versions of the story, it is Ayonwantha who combs the snakes out of Adodaroh's hair (cf. Mann's *Iroquoian Women*).

30. Mann, *Iroquoian Women*, 37.

31. Ibid., 118.

32. Mann, *Iroquoian Women*, 321.

33. Moon time refers to a woman's menstrual cycle.

34. Wakerahkats:teh, Clan Mother, interview by author, email message, August 24, 2015.

Chapter 4. Crossover Ceremonies

1. Wakerahkats:teh, Clan Mother, interview by author, email message, November 22, 2011.

2. Barreiro, ed., *Indian Roots of American Democracy*, 40–41.

3. Wakerahkats:teh, Clan Mother, interview by author, tape recording, Akwesasne, NY, May 27, 2012.

4. Ibid.

5. James Ransom, *Words That Come Before All Else* (New York: Native North American Travelling College), 141.

6. Iewirokwas, "Indian Time: A Voice from the Eastern Door," Grand Mother Moon, 2.

7. Wakerahkats:teh, Clan Mother, interview by author, tape recording, Akwesasne, NY, May 27, 2012.

8. Ibid.

9. Ibid.

10. Ibid.

11. For a baby to be considered veiled, it must be delivered covered with the amniotic sac.

12. Wakerahkats:teh, Clan Mother, interview by author, tape recording, Akwesasne, NY, May 27, 2012.

13. Iewirokwas, "Indian Time: A Voice from the Eastern Door," Grand Mother Moon, 2.

14. Wakerahkats:teh, Clan Mother, interview by author, email message, May 8, 2012.

15. Ibid. Additionally, it is at this time of her life cycle that a woman is able to be around any medicine, emanating from female or male. While in menses, women must stay with the blood side (other women) because otherwise

they would disturb the male medicine. The moon-time prohibition of men is a misunderstanding of this fact, aided by patriarchal hubris.

16. Ibid.

17. Mankiller, *Every Day Is a Good Day*, 35.

18. Wakerahkats:teh, Clan Mother, interview by author, email message, May 28, 2012.

19. Young man, interview by author, tape recording, Akwesasne, NY, May 20, 2012.

20. Young woman, interview by author, tape recording, Akwesasne, NY, May 20, 2012.

21. Clan Mother's words recorded by the author on May 16, 2014.

22. Wakerahkats:teh, Clan Mother, interview by author, tape recording, Akwesasne, NY, May 19, 2012.

23. Personal interview with Clan Mother on May 16, 2014.

24. Author's recording of the Clan Mother's speech, transcribed May 17, 2014.

25. Author's witness and recording of gathering, May 18, 2014.

26. Wakerahkats:teh, Clan Mother, interview by author, tape recording, Akwesasne, NY, May 15, 2014.

27. Clan Mother's Instructions to the Young Women during Their Preparation, March 17, 2011.

28. Women recite this from a printed Word document distributed by Clan Mother to participants.

29. Wakerahkats:teh, Clan Mother, interview by author, tape recording, Akwesasne, NY, May 19, 2014.

30. Wakerahkats:teh, Clan Mother, interview by author, tape recording, Akwesasne, NY, May 22, 2012.

31. Ibid.

32. Ibid.

33. Young woman 2, interview by author, tape recording, Akwesasne, NY, May 22, 2012.

34. Clan Mother's words, May 18, 2014.

35. Clan Mother's Instructions to the Young Men and Uncles during Their Preparation, March 18, 2011.

36. Personal communication with an uncle, June 1, 2014.

37. Young man, interview by author, tape recording, Akwesasne, NY, May 20, 2012.

38. Remarks from the mother of one of the young men going through the ceremony, May 20, 2014.

39. A young man's reflection, May 19, 2014.

40. Grandmother, interview by author, tape recording, Akwesasne, NY, May 15, 2014.

41. Curtis, *The North American Indian*, 22–23.

42. Wakerahkats:teh, Clan Mother, interview by author, tape recording, Akwesasne, NY, May 24, 2014.

Chapter 5. Indigenous Strategies in the Global Arena

1. Tonya Gonnella Frichner, "The State of the World's Indigenous Peoples," *Native Peoples Magazine* 23.5 (2010): 14.

2. "American Indian & Alaska Native Populations," Centers for Disease Control and Prevention, accessed September 12, 2015, http://www.cdc.gov/minorityhealth/populations/REMP/aian.html.

3. "Federal and State Recognized Tribes," The National Conference of State Legislatures, accessed September 12, 2015, http://www.ncsl.org/research/state-tribal-institute/list-of-federal-and-state-recognized-tribes.aspx.

4. Samir Amin, "Imperialism and Globalization," *The Monthly Review* 53.2 (2001).

5. State of the World's Indigenous Peoples, United Nations, New York, 2009, 85.

6. Amir, "Imperialism and Globalization," 14.

7. Alexander Ewen, ed., *Voice of Indigenous Peoples: Native People Address the United Nations* (Santa Fe: Clear Light, 1994), 33.

8. Ibid., 33–34.

9. Ibid., 134.

10. Ibid.

11. Ibid., 36.

12. Ibid., 35.

13. "Beyond Climate Change to Survival on Sacred Mother Earth," Address to the United Nations, September 21, 2014.

14. Ibid.

15. Cæcilie Mikkelsen, ed., *The Indigenous World 2013* (Copenhagen: The International Work Group for Indigenous Affairs, 2013), 48.

16. Saul Chernos, "The Mining Onslaught in Native Communities," *NOW Magazine*, May 2012.

17. Mikkelsen, ed., *The Indigenous World 2013*, 60.

18. Ibid., 56.

19. Wara Alderete, Gina Pacaldo, Xihuanel Huerta, and Lucilene Whitesell, eds., *Daughters of Abya Yala: Indigenous Women Regaining Control* (Summertown: Native Voices, 1992), 9.

20. Katsi Cook, "Women as the First Environment Collaborative," lecture at the Lifeblood of Our Nation's Gathering, Akwesasne, NY, August 27–29, 2010.

21. Alderete et al., *Daughters of Abya Yala*, 50–52.

22. "Madre Tierra, Madre Creadora," *Con-Spirando Revista Latinoamericana de ecofeminismo, espiritualidad y teologia* 2 (1992): 16–17.

23. Larry Rasmussen as quoted in Jeanette Rodriguez, "*La Tierra*: Home, Identity, and Destiny," in *From the Heart of Our People: Latino/a Explorations in Catholic Systematic Theology*, ed. Orlando O. Espin and Miguel H. Dias (New York: Orbis Books, 1999), 195.

24. Ewen, ed., *Voice of Indigenous Peoples*, 83.

25. "Madre Tierra, Madre Creadora," 16–17.

26. Mankiller, *Every Day Is a Good Day*, 5–6.

Conclusion

1. Ewen, ed., *Voice of Indigenous Peoples*, 128.

2. Duran, *Healing the Soul Wound*, 14.

3. Theodore W. Jennings, "On Ritual Knowledge," *Journal of Religion* 62 (1982): 112.

Works Cited

Akwesasne Notes, ed. *The Basic Call to Consciousness*. Rooseveltown, NY: Native Voices, 1978.

Alderete, Wara, Gina Pacaldo, Xihuanel Huerta, and Lucilene Whitesell, eds. *Daughters of Abya Yala: Indigenous Women Regaining Control*. Summertown: Book Publishing Company, 1992.

Alfred, Taiaiake. *Peace, Power, and Righteousness: An Indigenous Manifesto*. New York: Oxford University Press, 2009.

Amin, Samir. "Imperialism and Globalization." *The Monthly Review* 53.2 (2001): 6–24.

Anzaldúa, Gloria. *Borderlands: The New Mestiza*. Austin: University of Texas Press, 1987.

Barreiro, José, ed. *Indian Roots of American Democracy*. Ithaca: Cornell University Press, 1992.

"Beyond Climate Change to Survival on Sacred Mother Earth." Address to the United Nations. September 21, 2014.

Bockler, Carlos Guzman. "Memoria Colectiva: Identidad Histórica y Conciencia Étnica en Guatemala." *Revista Mexicana de Ciencias Políticas y Sociales* 27.103 (1981): 193–208.

Bodley, John. *Cultural Anthropology: Tribes, States and the Global System*. Mountain View: Mayfield, 2000.

Brammer, Leila R. *Excluded from Suffrage History: Matilda Joslyn Gage, Nineteenth-Century American Feminist*. London: Greenwood Press, 2000.

Chernos, Saul. "The Mining Onslaught in Native Communities." *NOW Magazine*, May 2012.

"The Constitution of the Iroquois Nations: The Great Binding Law, Gayanashagowa." Portland State University. Accessed June 13, 2014. http://www.iroquoisdemocracy.pdx.edu/html/greatlaw.html.

Cook, Katsi. "Women as the First Environment Collaborative." Lecture at The Lifeblood of Our Nation's Gathering. Akwesasne, NY, August 27–29, 2010.

Curtis, Edward S. *The North American Indian: The Complete Portfolios*. Cologne: Taschen Press, 1997.

Duran, Eduardo. *Healing the Soul Wound*. New York: Teachers College Press, 2006.

Duran, Eduardo, Judith Firehammer, and John Gonzalez. "Liberation Psychology as a Path towards Healing Cultural Soul Wounds." *The Journal of Counseling and Development* 86.3 (2011): 288–295.

Gurung, Jeannette. "Gender Dimensions of Biodiversity Management: Cases from Bhutan and Nepal." *Biodiversity in the Hindu Kush-Himalayas International Center for Integrated Mountain Development* 31 (1998): 98–107.

Ewen, Alexander, ed. *Voice of Indigenous Peoples: Native People Address the United Nations.* Santa Fe: Clear Light, 1994.

Mikkelsen, Cæcilie, ed. *The Indigenous World 2013.* Copenhagen: The International Work Group for Indigenous Affairs, 2013.

Frichner, Tonya Gonnella. "The State of the World's Indigenous Peoples." *Native Peoples Magazine* 23.5 (2010).

Hirsch, Herbert. *Genocide and the Politics of Memory.* Chapel Hill: University of North Carolina Press, 1995.

"The International Indigenous Women's Caucus at the World Women's Congress for a Healthy Planet." Native Web. Accessed May 24, 2014. http://www.nativeweb.org/papers/statements/women/healthyplanet.php.

Jacobs, Renee. "Iroquois Great Law of Peace and the United States Constitution: How the Founding Fathers Ignored Iakoiane Wakerakatste." *American Indian Law Review* 16.2 (1991): 497–531.

Jennings, Theodore W. "On Ritual Knowledge." *Journal of Religion* 62 (1982): 111–127.

Johansen, Bruce Elliott, and Barbara Alice Mann. *Encyclopedia of the Haudenosaunee (Iroquois Confederacy).* Westport, CT Greenwood, 2000.

Kanien'kehá:ka Council of Akwesasne. "What Is the Kanien'kehá:ka Council of Akwesasne?" Accessed January 15, 2014. http://www.akwesasne.ca/about.

"Madre Tierra, Madre Creadora." *Con-Spirando Revista Latinoamericana de ecofeminismo, espiritualidad y teologia* 2 (1992): 16–17.

Mankiller, Wilma. *Every Day Is a Good Day: Reflections by Contemporary Indigenous Women.* Golden: Fulcrum, 2004.

Mann, Barbara A. *Iroquoian Women: The Gantowisas.* New York: Peter Lang, 2006.

McMaster, Gerald, ed. *Native Universe: Voices of Indian America.* Washington, DC: The Smithsonian Institution, 2008.

Mikkelsen, Cæcilie, ed. *The Indigenous World 2013.* Copenhagen: The International Work Group for Indigenous Affairs, 2013.

Mohawk, John. *Iroquois Creation Story: John Arthur Gibson and J.N.B. Hewitt's Myth of the Earth Grasper.* N.p.: Mohawk Publications, 2005.

Mulvaney, Dustin, ed. *Green Politics: An A-to-Z Guide.* Los Angeles: Sage, 2011.

National Museum of the American Indian Education Office. "Haudenosaunee Guide for Educators." Washington, DC: Smithsonian Institution.

"Native Peoples of the Region: Oral Tradition." Great Lakes Information Network. Accessed February 14, 2014. http://www.great-lakes.net/teach/history/native/native_6.html.

Neihardt, John G. *Black Elk Speaks*. Albany: State University of New York Press, 2008.

Paul, Elsie, Paige Rabmon, and Harmony Johnson. *Written as I Remember It: Teachings from the Life of a Sliammon Elder*." Vancouver: University of British Columbia Press, 2015.

Porter, Tom. *And Grandma Said . . . Iroquois Teachings as Passed Down through the Oral Tradition*. Cornwall, ON: Xlibris Corporation, 2008.

Porter, Tom. *Clanology: Clan System of the Iroquois*. New York: Native North American Travelling College, 1993.

Ransom, James. *Words That Come Before All Else*. New York: Native North American Travelling College.

Rawson, George. "We Limit Not the Truth of God." In *The New Century Hymnal*. Cleveland: Pilgrim Press, 1995.

Rockwell, Joan E. "The Meaning of Old Age from Native American Haudenosaunee (Iroquois) Women's Perspective: Then and Now." Unpublished master's thesis.

Rodriguez, Jeanette. "*La Tierra*: Home, Identity, and Destiny." In *From the Heart of Our People: Latino/a Explorations in Catholic Systematic Theology*, ed. Orlando O. Espin and Miguel H. Dias, 189–208. New York: Orbis Books, 1999.

Rodriguez, Jeanette, and Ted Fortier. *Cultural Memory: Resistance, Faith and Identity*. Austin: University of Texas Press, 2007.

Simpson, Leanne R. "Anticolonial Strategies for the Recovery and Maintenance of Indigenous Knowledge." *American Indian Quarterly* 28.3–4 (Summer and Fall 2010): 373–384.

"State of the World's Minorities and Indigenous Peoples 2012." United Nations Press. Accessed February 15, 2014. http://www.unesco.org/library/PDF/MRG.pdf.

"VI Latin America Encounter of Pastoral and Solidarity Work with Indigenous Peoples." *Journal of Promotio Iustitiae* 2 (2006): 33–40.

Swamp, Chief Jake. "Remembering the Ancient Path: The Original Instructions and the Earth Charter." In *A Voice for Earth: American Writers Respond to the Earth Charter*, ed. A. James Wohlpart and Peter Blaze Corcoran, 54–60. Athens: University of Georgia Press, 2008.

Syracuse Peace Council. "Who Are the Haudenosaunee?" Accessed June 15, 2014. http://www.peacecouncil.net/NOON/culture1.html.

"Tribal Names and Meanings." Native History Memory. Accessed May 8, 2014. http://www.nativehistorymagazine.com/2013/01/tribal-names-and-their-meanings.html.

Venables, Robert. *The Clearing and the Woods: The Haudenosaunee (Iroquois) Landscape—Gendered and Balanced*. Philadelphia: Springer Press, 2010.

Wagner, Sally Roesch. "Haudenosaunee Women: An Inspiration to Early Feminists." In *Sisters in Spirit*. Summertown: Native Voices, 2001.

Wallace, Paul. *The Iroquois Book of Life: White Roots of Peace*. Santa Fe: Clear Light, 1986.

Willow, Anna J. "Images of American Indians in Environmental Education: Anthropological Reflections on the Politics and History of Cultural Representation." *American Educational Research Journal* 34.1 (2010): 67–88.

Wohlpart, A. James, and Peter Blaze Corcoran, eds. *A Voice for Earth: American Writers Respond to Earth Charter*. Athens: University of Georgia Press, 2008.

About the Authors

Left: Bear Clan Mother Wakerahkats:teh, right: the Author, Jeanette Rodriguez

IAKOIANE WAKERAHKATS:TEH is a Condoled Bear Clan Mother from the Kanien'kehá:ka (Mohawk) Nation at Akwesasne. She is also a third-generation Bear Clan Matron, keeper of the Chieftainship title (Tehanakari:ne). A longtime advocate for the preservation of the Kanien'kehá:ka language, her recent work centers on women's wellness and the restoration of puberty rites for the youth within her community. She has traveled to the United Nations advocating the rights of indigenous men and women.

JEANETTE RODRIGUEZ is a professor at Seattle University and teaches in the Department of Theology and Religious Studies, Women Studies, and the Graduate School of Theology and Ministry. Rodriguez is the author of several books and articles concentrated in the areas of US/Latino/a religious experience, theologies of liberation, cultural memory, women and spirituality, and peace building. Her works include *Our Lady of Guadalupe: Faith and Empowerment among Mexican-American Women*, *Stories We Live*, *Cultural Memory: Resistance, Faith and Identity* (coauthored with Ted Fortier), and *A Reader in Latina Feminist Theology* (coedited with Maria Pilar Aquino and Daisy Machado). She has served as board member for the Academy of Hispanic Theologians in the United States and as vice chair for Pax Christi USA. Presently, she is on the board of the NCR. Rodriguez holds a PhD in Religion and the Personality Sciences from the Graduate Theological Union, Berkeley, California (1990).

Index